Upkeep of Greenhouses

Upkeep of Greenhouses

Don't Just Mow Your Lawn... Manicure it with a Mantis Reel Mower. It's the green, clean, quiet solution to maintaining smaller lawns!

Here are 7 advantages of owning a Mantis Reel Mower for your lawn:

> **Better Cut.** Reel mowers shear each blade like a pair of scissors. A sheared cut yields a greener and healthier lawn, and is preferred by lawn care professionals.

> **Quiet.** You can cut the lawn anytime without disturbing the neighbors or the wildlife. You can actually hear the birds while you cut the lawn!

> **Non-polluting.** The savings in fuel is significant to both the environment and your wallet. Plus, no more dead spark plugs, messy oil changes or stored fuel.

> **Lightweight.** Today's Mantis Reel Mowers are lighter, easier to push and more effective than the old push mowers.

> **Low Maintenance.** Aside from the occasional drop of oil and blade sharpening, there's little maintenance required. Our blades are made of hardened steel which do not require yearly sharpening.

> **Inexpensive.** Why buy a more expensive gas mower when you can have a better looking yard, a much more enjoyable mowing experience, and take time to smell the grass!

> **One-Year, Risk-Free Trial** – The Mantis Promise – Try the Mantis Reel Mower that you buy directly from Mantis with absolutely NO RISK! If you're not completely satisfied, send it back to us within ONE YEAR for a COMPLETE, NO-HASSLE REFUND.

Upkeep of Greenhouses

Contents

How Does A Greenhouse Capture Heat?

A greenhouse uses a special kind of glass that acts as a medium which selectively transmits spectral frequencies. Spectral comes from the word "spectrum".

In layman's terms, a spectral frequency can be defined in terms of the following principle: any object in the universe emits, radiates or transmits light. The distribution of this light along an electromagnetic spectrum is determined by the object's composition.

Therefore, the glass of a greenhouse traps energy within the greenhouse and the heat in turn provides heat for the plants and the ground inside the greenhouse. It warms the air near the ground, preventing it from rising and leaving the confines of the structure.

For example, if you open a small window near the roof of a greenhouse, the temperature drops significantly. This is because of the auto vent automatic cooling system. An autovent is simply a device used by greenhouses that maintain a range of temperatures inside. This is how greenhouses trap electromagnetic radiation and prevents convection (transference of heat by currents within a fluid).

Curious about how the idea of a greenhouse came about? It goes back to the days of the Romans, who - as history annals show - were the first people to create a structure to protect plants. Using heated pits, they put up slabs of rock to form primitive greenhouses. The term "glasshouse" which is the correct name of this structure, was adopted sometime in the 17th and 18th centuries.

At that time, however, the error was in believing that heat was more important than light for plants to thrive. Structures were being built to exclude the entry of light, but by the time the glass tax of 1845 was abolished, the design of greenhouses started to change.

Builders realized then that a curved roof instead of a flat one allowed higher concentrations of the sun's rays, and that by using iron instead of wood, the greenhouse could be structurally reinforced and made capable of absorbing more light.

Types Of Greenhouses

After you decide that you want to build a greenhouse, you have to decide next what type to build. This should not be a difficult one to address, provided you know what kinds of plants you want to grow. You will need to answer questions such as:

ð	What will my greenhouse be principally used for?

ð	Do I want a large or small greenhouse?

ð	Will the greenhouse be the main attraction of my garden?

ð	Is my garden exposed to strong winds?

ð	Are there young children or wild animals in the area?

Factors such as cost and space will determine the type of greenhouse you build. If you do live in a windy area, it may be worth to spend the extra money for a solid and sturdy greenhouse. If you live near a large hardware store or a nursery, or even a do-it-yourself home center, go and visit some models. The customer service representative should be able to provide you with valuable information before you make a final decision.

So as not to mislead you, while there may be different types of greenhouse designs, we're talking about the same greenhouse. You get to decide which type you want it to be. For example, if temperature is the main factor, because of the plant varieties you want to grow, then there are three types in terms of temperature control. There are also different types of greenhouses based on structural design. We'll start with temperature control factors.

For temperature control purposes, three types of greenhouses exist:

ð	a hot greenhouse
ð	 a warm greenhouse
ð	a cool greenhouse.

Tools And Materials For Your Greenhouse

Remember that you are not limited to a certain variety of plants to grow in a greenhouse. Bear in mind, however, that your preference for certain fruits, vegetables and plants will determine the type of greenhouse you like to build. "Know thy crop" is an important factor before deciding on the greenhouse type you will install.

You will need a good soil for planting seeds. Compost, potting or gardening soil and a little sand or perlite are a good start. Read all directions in your seed packets.

Keep some of those black plastic flats that nurseries use to display their plant containers. These are useful for starting sees and transplants.

Benches in greenhouses are essential, as they hold trays of plants that have already sprouted from seeds.

Styrofoam cups - have several of these handy. Seeds sprout quickly and once they grow large enough to move into separate containers, they can be gently lifted and transferred into ordinary Styrofoam cups.

You can also use yogurt plastic cups, and large commercial type containers that can hold more than one plant. In fact, any container you can think of will be suitable.

Other materials you should have on hand are broken clay pots, cracked walnuts, marbles, charcoal or gravel. These help in proper drainage. Be sure to soak clay pots in water a few minutes before using them. This will prevent the clay from absorbing the moisture from the potting soil.

If you want to have trellises inside your greenhouse, you can make them out of coat hangers, which you can bend to any shape your heart desires.

Herbs are perfect for keeping pests at bay. They are what one writer calls "nature's insecticides". Have a variety of them inside your greenhouse. You can make a natural insecticide by adding onions or garlic to a jar of water. Leave it for a week and spray on your plants.

Other garden tools that will help you run your greenhouse efficiently are air coolers for the hot summer. This is to maintain the temperatures at desired levels.   Power vents in the roof are also a good idea to release hot air that can build up suddenly in the summer.

Greenhouse Tables, Shelving And Plant Holders

These are indispensable, especially when you need to work inside your greenhouse and to maximize and organize your greenhouse space. As your plant varieties grow, you will need shelves and tables and plant holders to facilitate your gardening. One popular type of bench that greenhouse hobbyists like is the cedar double layer bench. They are durable and efficient to use.

For shelves, you can opt for two and three section lengths made of aluminum

Given that watering your plants is an essential - indispensable -part of any greenhouse gardening, a good watering system is required. You can choose either the automatic or hand held watering system to make your watering needs more efficient.

For automatic irrigation systems, there are models that come equipped with an automatic drip irrigation and fertilizer system. Day or night, they regularly water the plants and adjust the flow of fertilizer. Some have a tank in which the water and fertilizer are mixed and are distributed to plants via hoses, Y-connections and drip pins.

Greenhouse garden coil indoor/outdoor watering wand

This is a "self-coiling" garden hose made of rugged and durable polyurethane tubing. It produces ultra-fine mists and sprays in soft, gentle streams. Some wand models extend to as long as 50 feet. No hassle storage because of self-coiling mechanism.

Greenhouses constantly evolve in style and design. It follows then that tools and accessories will grow in number or existing ones will be considerably improved. Manufacturers are probably inventing more tools and accessories this very moment that will make our work in greenhouses easier and quicker.

The ones we just described are already being used by many greenhouse enthusiasts. In a few years, new products will definitely appear in the market.

Tips For Your Greenhouse

If you're growing carrots, beets, turnips and other root crops, they thrive well in deep boxes which can be put under benches. Those that require tub-type containers are tomatoes, peas, cucumbers and pole beans, while lettuce, or other low leafy vegetables may be planted in the tub with the taller vegetables.

You can plant corn directly on the floor of the greenhouse, in a special bed prepared for it. To save space, you can plant pumpkin between the rows of corn.

Use room temperature water to water your indoor plants. Let tap water stand for a day to get rid of the chlorine substance. This way you avoid your plants getting brown tips.

Distribute crushed egg shells in your garden to stimulate growth. Sprinkling coffee grounds will add acid to the greenhouse ground.

Before bringing vegetables and fruits from the greenhouse to your house, rinse them well outside; this way dirt and bugs stay outside and will not make your kitchen dirty.

To make more room in your greenhouse, use lower benches for starting seeds and transplants; upper benches for growing flowers and specimen plants. Some vegetables, like tomatoes, should be planted in a warm section of the greenhouse.

Regarding planting of seeds, be sure to water lightly for the first few times. Over watering may cause the seeds to come to the surface too soon, preventing them from rooting properly.

Preparation and production must be done in separate areas. Don't do general preparation on the growing floor. This makes for a tidier greenhouse.

Here is a list of the largest vegetables that will need the most spacing in your greenhouse:

ð   bush type beans: minimum of five feet between rows,

- ð   cabbage: a foot between rows,

- ð   peppers: about a foot between rows,

- ð   cantaloupes: two to three feet between rows,

- ð   squash: two to three feet between rows,

- ð   tomatoes and watermelons: minimum of two feet between rows.

Learn The Benefits Of Greenhouse Gardening

Greenhouse gardening can seem a little old fashioned these days. It is so easy to jump in the car and drive to the supermarket where we can find every kind of fruit and vegetables flown in from all over the world. You want fresh strawberries in winter? No problem, there they are on the shelf. May be you need some green beans for dinner. Pick up a little plastic wrapped tray that were growing three days ago in Kenya.

But these are the very reasons for moving to greenhouse gardening. Driving and flying burn up increasingly scarce fossil fuels and release greenhouse gases into the atmosphere. More and more people are waking up to the dangers of global warming.

Fresh fruit and vegetables have never been easier to buy than they are today. We live in an age of convenience and immediate gratification. A greenhouse seems to entail just too much work and the gratification is postponed for too long. Greenhouses seem pointless until we begin to think about the wider picture and the kind of world our children and grandchildren will inherit.

Getting into greenhouse gardening can be an ecologically and socially responsible choice. You will be eating fruit and vegetables that have grown in your own backyard. They have not been flown half way round the planet to get to your plate. What's more you did not have to drive to get them. You took a short walk and got some healthy exercise every day when you walked out to the greenhouse to check on them.

We have got used to those convenient little packages in the supermarket. We like the idea of having our vegetables ready prepared and washed. But we have also got used to poor taste. The fruit and vegetables we buy in the supermarket have lost most of their natural sugars that give them their flavor. Even the varieties are chosen for their shelf life rather than their flavor.

When you experience home grown fruit and vegetables fresh from the greenhouse you will enter another quality of flavor. A fresh picked tomato explodes in your mouth with flavor. Growing your own in the greenhouse means that you can select varieties that have the best flavor.

A whole range of unusual varieties exist that are rarely grown commercially are available to you with a greenhouse. With your own greenhouse you can explore these lesser known varieties of familiar fruit and vegetables. You can even become really adventurous and try the kinds of fruit and vegetables that you only get in specialist stores.

A greenhouse opens the world to you rather than bringing it to you at great cost to the planet and everyone on it. Your carbon footprint will be smaller but your horizons will be wider.

"But I don't have time." I hear you say and it is true we are all short of time. But a little time spent in the greenhouse has enormous personal benefits. It is incredibly therapeutic to go into the greenhouse after a hard day and just work quietly for an hour or so. Spending time with growing things is a recognized antidote to depression and anxiety. A greenhouse is a tranquilizer with no side effects except a healthier diet.

If you have kids, what better way to spend some quality time with them than in the greenhouse. It gives you and them unpressured time to talk. You are engaged in a joint task. A greenhouse can become a bonding experience for the family.

There is the added benefit that working with you in the greenhouse gives them the kind of practical hands on lesson that is seldom provided in school. They are learning about how things grow. Each session in the greenhouse is a biology lesson in itself. They are learning about the plants and about the insects that feed on them and pollinate them.

They, and you, will learn a lot about organic chemistry when you mix your plant foods, insecticides and other chemicals. You will undoubtedly learn a lot about electronics and handling basic tools as you get the control systems of your greenhouse working and rig up plant supports and irrigation pipes.

A child who finds academic lessons a difficult will often shine at tasks they can learn by experience. Plants are very forgiving and even children who suffer with problems of concentration can experience the satisfaction of achievement growing a few simple crops in the greenhouse.745

Managing The Greenhouse Climate

Managing the climate of a greenhouse is about providing the plants with the right conditions for growth, flowering and fruiting. What you need to do will therefore depend on the kind of plants you are growing and the stage they have reached in their life cycle.

Not all plants need exactly the same conditions so the kind of climate will depend on what you plan to grow in you greenhouse. Some will need high temperatures and high humidity in the greenhouse. Others will require slightly cooler conditions in the greenhouse.

It is often possible to reach a compromise and provide conditions that will suit most of your plants most of the time. You will not be able to provide optimum conditions for all the plants in your greenhouse. But by choosing plants that like similar conditions you will achieve acceptable results.

For the amateur greenhouse grower some compromises are necessary. If you are growing commercially that is another matter. A commercial greenhouse must provide an optimum climate for a specific type of plant. Otherwise you will lose money.

An amateur who is dedicated to a particular species has to make some hard choices. It may be necessary to sacrifice variety for quality. If your greenhouse is devoted to orchids and only orchids you can provide the best climatic conditions. If you want to grow other types of plant you will just have to build another greenhouse.

For most gardeners such hard decisions are not necessary. It is possible to provide a climate that will suit many plants to some extent. You may also find that you can partition off part of the greenhouse to create a microclimate. Part of the greenhouse can then have a climate that is hotter or more humid than the rest.

In a temperate part of the planet where there is a relatively long growing season it is often possible to have an unheated greenhouse. An unheated greenhouse relies on the sun's rays and the residual heat stored in the ground to create a climate that is warmer than the outside environment. This is adequate for raising seeds and for growing vegetables such as tomatoes in the summer.

Regulating the climate in an unheated greenhouse is mainly a matter of making sure that there is enough humidity to avoid pests such as white fly and red spider mite and enough ventilation to avoid mildew and botritus. The lower the Temperature the lower the humidity should be. Air cannot hold much moisture at low temperature and rot will result if the greenhouse is not properly ventilated.

Providing some heat will allow a longer growing season. If the greenhouse is heated in the winter it will be possible to provide a frost-free space for tender plants that live outdoors in the summer. A small amount of heat will provide a greenhouse climate in which some salads can be grown all fear round.

The simplest method of achieving a frost free greenhouse is the old fashioned one of placing a candle in a large plant pot with another one over the top. The plant pots heat up and continue to give out heat through the night. Your greenhouse will be frost free in several degrees of frost. If you intend to keep your greenhouse heated all day or if the climate in your region is very cold in winter you will need to invest in a more complex form of heating. Electric heating is by far the best option. It can be thermostatically regulated to produce exactly the climate you need.

Electric heating is expensive, but you can reduce heat loss by insulating your greenhouse with bubble wrap plastic. This is the same kind of material that is used in packaging. You can buy it in big sheets from garden suppliers. When it is clipped to the inside of the greenhouse it creates a double glazed environment.

Insulating a greenhouse allows you to maintain higher temperatures in your greenhouse. But you must be careful about humidity. Some ventilation will still be necessary. Venting the greenhouse in the middle of the day will control the internal climate. Cheaper forms of heating exist but any kind of combustion inevitably produces gases that are harmful to plants. They are best avoided. If you have plenty of wood then you might consider a wood burning stove. Rather than put such a stove directly in the greenhouse it would be better to use it as a central heating stove and pipe hot water through your greenhouse.

Gardening Inside The Greenhouse

A greenhouse represents a major investment for most gardeners. Even the smallest and simplest types of greenhouse do not come cheap these days. They also demand an investment of your time. So why should you consider a greenhouse.

Perhaps the main advantage of a greenhouse is that is provides the gardener with a longer growing season. This is particularly important in colder areas. A greenhouse will provide an early start for seedlings, warmer conditions for tender plants and a frost free environment for plants that will not survive out of doors.

Another, less often recognized, advantage is that a greenhouse allows a gardener with mobility problems to garden at table height in warm conditions. Plants can be raised to a convenient height for the gardener in a greenhouse. Simple staging, either home made or bought for the purpose will create an environment in which a disabled gardener can enjoy all the pleasures of gardening without having to bend or stretch or get chilled.

A greenhouse can become a favorite place to sit and enjoy the rest of your garden. On a cold winter day the greenhouse will keep the wind of and provide a sheltered spot to think about next year's plans.

What you use a greenhouse for will depend on your own personal preferences. Beautiful displays of alpines can be created in a greenhouse on benches covered with gravel. It may seem strange to grow plants that are essentially hardy in a greenhouse but it makes sense. Alpines hate to get wet. They are used to being frozen all winter but will not survive damp conditions. Their flowers are often small and can best be appreciated when placed on a bench.

Summer bedding plants and vegetable seeds can be raised in an unheated greenhouse. If you want to avoid paying high prices for ready grown plants a greenhouse may be the answer. You can grow many more plants from a packet of seeds than you could afford to buy. Your garden will become a riot of color as you experiment with new annual bedding schemes, hanging baskets and planters.

Vegetables will reach maturity earlier if you raise you seeds in a greenhouse. Your crops will be ready before out door sown plants are ready for harvesting. With all plants sown in the greenhouse you must be careful to harden them to outdoor conditions slowly. Put them outside when the risk of frost has passed. Do this during the day at first. As they get used to the colder conditions you can leave them out at night. When you are sure they are strong enough plant them in their final position.

By this time you will be ready to think about what you want to grow in your greenhouse during the summer. You may wish to grow fruit and vegetables. Tomatoes and cucumbers or melons are always favorites. They are comparatively easy to grow. All of these can be grown without heat.

If you want to use your greenhouse in the winter you must provide heating. Perhaps the best form of heating in a small amateur greenhouse is an electric heater. This can be controlled by a thermostat which will regulate the temperature in the greenhouse. The thermostat can be set at the desired temperature. Regulating the temperature is the best way to keep a check on the cost of heating.

For over wintering plants that grow outside in the summer but are not winter hardy the temperature only needs to be set just above freezing. A few degrees of warmth will maintain tender plants in a semi-dormant state until you can return them to the garden.

To continue using your greenhouse for plants and flowers that are in growth you will need higher temperatures. Summer plants can be grown all year round in this way. If you are going to heat your greenhouse to growing temperatures around 60 or 70 degrees Fahrenheit you should think about insulating the greenhouse with bubble wrap plastic.

It may be necessary to provide additional lighting if you are at a northern latitude with short winter day lengths. Plants need light in addition to warmth and humidity. Plants need light as well as warmth. Some of them need specific day lengths before they come into flower. Lighting allows you to control the condition completely. This is how commercial growers bring flowers into bloom in time for Christmas.

Greenhouse Kits For Plant Enthusiasts

Even the simplest greenhouse can be expensive and ready made ones are seldom just what we want. A ready made greenhouse may not fit our plot or may not provide quite enough space for what we plan to grow. Constructing your own greenhouse from a kit may the best option for many gardeners.

So if you are working to a tight budget or dream of a custom designed greenhouse a kit may be just the thing you need. The level of skill involved is within the range of most of us. If you can carry out simple tasks around the home and follow basic instructions then you can probably assemble a greenhouse from a kit.

First of all you must think about what you want from your greenhouse. How must it look? If you want an elegant design that is going to look good, then one of the redwood greenhouse kits may the thing for you. Take a look at the Sunshine range. These are made from solid redwood frames with polycarbonate glazing.

This type of greenhouse kit is easy to assemble because the glazing is built into the frame, so you have no cutting to do. Cutting glass is a tricky business. Fitting glass into a frame is even more difficult and you may have many broken panes before you succeed in getting a good fit. Polycarbonate is also safe. This is especially important when there are children about.

Redwood greenhouse kits are good choice. The drawback is their cost. They range from $1000 to $4000.

If budget is an important consideration for you take a look at aluminum framed greenhouse kits. These range in price from $2,500 to £30,000. At the lower end of the range you may find a design that suits your needs. They are less elegant than the redwood greenhouse kits but Cross Country range are very well designed and will provide years of gardening service.

Priced at $1000 to $2000 there is the Hobby Gardener range of greenhouse kits. These have "snaplass" panels made of polycarbonate. They provide a good height that makes working in them easy and plenty of space for the plants. Their hinged door and vent system allow the gardener to create an ideal microclimate inside the greenhouse.

In terms of features such as doors and venting aluminum and readwood kits are comparable. They are engineered to high standards. An aluminum frame greenhouse will never look as beautiful as a redwood one but they have the advantage that the frame needs no maintenance. Once an aluminum greenhouse is built that is all you have to do. from the gardener's point of view they are trouble free.

Also good for those with limited budgets is the Juliana range of greenhouse kits. These are made of aluminum frames and have twin wall polycarbonate glazing. They start as low as $65 making them an ideal choice for the price conscious. For those on a really tight budget the Little Greenhouse range of kits may be the ideal option. These greenhouse kits are covered with four millimeter polyethylene sheeting on a PVC frame. They are less durable than the types of greenhouse kits already discussed but they are more economical and good for the beginner.

If you are not yet sure if you want to make a big investment of time and money then a Little Greenhouse kit may be a good starting point. Perhaps you do not intend to stay long at your present home and do not want to commit to an expensive structure. They are even useful if you already have a more permanent greenhouse but want that extra bit of space. This kind of greenhouse kit may be the ideal one for all kinds of reasons.

If you need to cover a large area and the appearance of the structure is not important to you then you could try a portable greenhouse. These are made of a steel frame covered with plastic sheeting. You can get these for as little as $300. They look like the commercial polytunnels they are but the hobby gardener can put them to good use. Inside you can create a tropical paradise if you use a double layer of polythene.

Polythene is always a cheap option for a greenhouse kit. But is does not have the durability of polycarbonate or the light transmission properties. A polythene cover will need to be changed every year or so. Polycarbonate will last for years. In addition twin walled polycarbonate reduces heating costs because it provides insulation and ensures less heat loss to the outside environment.

Create A Warm And Suitable Environment For Growth With Greenhouse Plastic

Plastic in all its many forms has largely replaced glass in the garden. Not only is it safer, an important consideration when there are children about, but it has better thermal properties and often transmits more light.

What you are trying to achieve by using greenhouse plastic is a microclimate suited to your plants. You are protecting them from the rigors of the outside environment. You are keeping them safe from frost, low temperatures, wind and rain.

In a windswept spot the gardener can use greenhouse plastic to protect plants from dehydration caused by the wind. In a temperate but damp climate a well ventilated greenhouse will allow alpines which prefer cold dry conditions and good light to thrive. In northern latitudes the same materials can be used for tropical and semi-tropical plants or to give hardy plants an early start.

The advantage of modern plastic materials is that the same greenhouse technology can be applied widely in the garden. There is no need to confine yourself to a traditional greenhouse structure. You may use greenhouse plastic in a temporary structure that covers part of the garden for a few months of the year. Equally you can use plastic to construct an elaborate permanent greenhouse.

The most widely used plastics are PVC, polyethylene and copolymers. Each of these types of plastic has its own properties and uses. They all be cut easily and do not shatter which used to be the problem with glass in the greenhouse. This allows them to be used in innovative structures or customized to fit awkward spaces.

When choosing plastic for a greenhouse it is important to opt for a high grade material that will withstand wear and tear. Low grade plastic will deteriorate when exposed to the environment and become increasingly opaque. The plastic used in a greenhouse must transmit light well. Some plastics may need to be replaced after a year. So go for a plastic that is specifically designed for greenhouse use. It will last longer.

Plastic that is going to be used in a greenhouse needs to be resistant to degradation by ultraviolet radiation. Many plastics are weakened by ultraviolet radiation and will tear easily over time.

If you want long term use out of plastic sheeting choose a reinforced type. This is especially important if wind damage is a question. Alternatively use a rigid plastic. Twin wall polycarbonate is an ideal choice for a more permanent structure. It has the added advantage of providing insulation because air is trapped between the two walls.

When used in a conventional greenhouse twin wall polycarbonate looks like glass but will reduce your heating bills. It is a kind of instant double glazing. It has brought down the cost of greenhouse gardening and brought the genuine hot house within the reach of the hobby gardener. It is no longer prohibitively expensive to heat your greenhouse to high temperatures in the winter.

Plastic has really revolutionized greenhouse construction. No where is this more true than with flexible plastic sheeting. This material has allowed crops like strawberries to be grown all the year round even in northern latitudes. Polytunnels have become widespread in commercial horticulture.

The same commercial technology is increasingly becoming available to the hobbyist. It is possible to buy the same steel frame, plastic sheeting that the professionals use. The frames produce a free standing tunnel structure over which plastic is stretched and secured with special clips. A range of sizes are available and the smaller sizes are ideal for amateur use.

A tunnel of this type allows a large area to be covered comparatively cheaply. An entire vegetable plot can be covered in this way very economically.

Perhaps the main advantage of such a structure is its temporary nature. The whole thing can be dismantled and moved or stored away until next year. The hobbyist then has the advantage of a greenhouse without having to devote part of the plot to a structure that is only used to the full for a short part of the year.

A tunnel shaped steel frame covered in plastic is not the most beautiful object. Many people would prefer to keep it out sight of the house. But it provides enormous and still largely unexplored possibilities for ornamental subjects. A double layer of plastic will provide insulation. Temperatures can then be brought up to hot house levels and a range of tropical plants grown.

It is possible to create a naturalistic tropical environment in this way. A small water feature will raise the humidity and allow the plants to grow in a way that they never can in the dry environment of a house. Fish and other creatures can be added to complete the tropical scene.

By using modern plastic materials you can create a greenhouse environment that would once have been beyond the budget of most people.

Greenhouses: Where The Grass Is Green All Year-Round

The winter comes. The nights draw in and we forget the decking and the patio until the spring. But in the greenhouse it is summer all year. With a greenhouse it is possible to have a little piece of summer that stays with us through the dark winter evenings and the snow.

Heating a greenhouse used to be an expensive business. But with modern materials that is no longer true. It is now possible to heat a greenhouse quite economically. What was once a luxury is available to everyone.

A twin wall polycarbonate greenhouse is double glazed and will keep in the heat. You can use an electric heater that is controlled by a thermostat. Very little heat will escape into the outside environment. By carefully regulating the temperature it is possible to keep the bills under control.

If you keep the temperature a little above freezing you can grow plants that like fairly cool temperature. A display of cyclamen, for example, would be a delight. When we keep them in our homes they easily get too hot. A frost free greenhouse would be ideal for them. You can bring one or two in to the house for a day or two before returning them to the greenhouse to be revived in the cooler temperature.

There are a whole range of plants that are sold as house plants but really hate the dry atmosphere. Think of all those lovely plants that die after a few weeks. Crotons with their beautiful leaves or Schizanthus, the poor man's orchid or butterfly flower, as it is sometimes known, they love humidity. In a greenhouse you can give them the conditions they need.

Many spectacular plants, such as the bird of paradise flower, or the strelizia, only need night time temperature of 55 degrees Fahrenheit. That is not hard to achieve. In the day time the sun will raise the temperature for you. You will need day time heating on only a few days of the year.

Put one of your garden chairs in the greenhouse and sit there in the winter sun listening to some music surrounded by flowers and greenery. The great thing about a greenhouse is you can use it pretty much however you want.

I know people who keep fish in their greenhouses. A small pool easily freezes over if you have hard winters in your part of the world. You can lose your fish that way. In the greenhouse the water stays free of ice and you can feed your prize koi carp right through the winter.

Interior designers often talk about bringing the garden into the house. Well, with a greenhouse you are really intermingling garden and house. Your greenhouse can become a room devoted to plants or an extension of the garden.

But maybe the kitchen is more your thing and you want to grow fruit and vegetable crops in your greenhouse. You want the taste of fresh picked produce right through the winter. That can be done too.

You can grow all kinds of crops in you greenhouse. Salads are probably the easiest of all. Fresh lettuce, rocket, spinach and other leaves can be grown on a cut and come again basis. Herbs can be done the same way. All you have to do when you want to make a salad is to pop out to the greenhouse and pull a few leaves.

Salad takes on another dimension when it is that fresh. Just keep a raincoat or an umbrella by the kitchen door. Tomatoes are also simple to grow through the winter. They need heat. They like to be about 70 degrees.

You should also think about lighting if you want to grow crops in the winter. Most fruit and vegetables need longer day lengths than a northern winter allows. Fluorescent lights are fairly good and cheap to run but you will get the best results from grolights that mimic the spectrum of natural daylight. They are metal halide or high pressure sodium lights that have a reflector to increase the amount of light. You can also make reflectors to go round the plants from ordinary aluminum baking foil. That can be a goof idea even when you are relying on sunlight in the winter.

Whatever you are growing in your greenhouse you must think about ventilation. You need the air to move through the greenhouse. In the winter when you want to conserve heat this can be done with a ventilation fan. They are not unlike the ones used in kitchens and bathrooms or in cooker hoods. You can modify one of those if you are handy with tools or buy one that is purpose made for the greenhouse.

If you really want to conserve heat you can fit a flexible hose to the vent and feed the expelled air back into the greenhouse. For extra effect you can run the hose into a pit filled with black rocks. The warm air will heat up the rocks which will act as a storage heater, slowly giving off heat through the night.

So whether you go for a greenhouse that is a place to sit and watch the plants and fish or a greenhouse that is intended to produce crops there are good reasons to think about greenhouse gardening.

What Makes Up The Greenhouse Structure?

The construction of greenhouses has been revolutionized by the advent of modern plastics. A range of possibilities are available that would have been unknown in the past.

Greenhouses were once made of wood and glass and even cast iron and glass. These materials represented a dramatic technological development in their time. Now these traditional materials are a rarity. They are preserved in the grounds of stately homes and classic botanical gardens.

The arrival of aluminum made greenhouses available to a wider market after World War Two. They were still glazed with glass and comparatively expensive. But the demand for the hobby greenhouse had begun.

While high quality hobby greenhouses are often made of quality timber such as redwood the most common type of greenhouse structure for the amateur is made of aluminum. A timber frame will always look better. The aesthetics of the aluminum structure reveal its origins in commercial horticulture. To many people they are unappealing, if functional.

Commercial greenhouses are still often based on aluminum structures, but the glazing material has changed. Greenhouses are usually glazed with twin wall polycarbonate these days. This material has the advantage that is cheaper than glass and does not shatter. It also provides better thermal insulation than glass. The air trapped between the two walls keeps warmth from escaping into the outside environment.

Even the frame of a greenhouse may be made of plastic. The potential of UPVC, a rigid plastic material that is resistant to ultraviolet radiation, was first recognized in the construction industry. It is employed for doors and double glazed windows. The same system has now spread to greenhouses. Standard units of double glazing, or made to measure panels, are made in a factory and brought to the site where they can be bolted together.

The use of new materials has allowed new designs of greenhouse structure to be explored. A greenhouse used to be a rectangular structure often with a pitched roof. This was a practical design and is still widely used. But the dome shaped greenhouse has become increasingly popular. Often called a solar dome, this type of structure makes the most use of light.

Dome shaped greenhouses were constructed out of cast iron in the nineteenth century. They were a great luxury. They were often used as palm houses. Surviving examples are spectacular and rare structures.

Aluminum allowed dome shaped greenhouse to be mass produced for the first time. The same shape can now be found in redwood frames too. Greenhouses of this type are often used as sun rooms and to cover pools in cold climates. On a vast scale the same concept of a dome shape has been for the famous Eden Project biomes in Britain. The framework of these structures is made of steel. Three giant dome shaped greenhouses cover a reclaimed china clay pit and provide a series of environments that reflect the diversity of the planet.

No less visually spectacular, in its own way, is the humble polytunnel. This is a greenhouse structure made of plastic sheeting stretched over a steel framework. Greenhouses of this type are widely used commercially. There are so many of them in Southern Spain that they can be seen from space. Satellite pictures show large areas of the region carpeted with polytunnels.

Their commercial uses are obvious but they the polytunnel can also be used in the same way as the more spectacular greenhouses of the Eden Project. The Alternative Technology Centre in Wales has a polytunnel planted with a range of tropical plants. A small water feature provides humidity for the plants. The whole effect is of a peaceful and lush tropical environment.

At a simpler level the use of plastics has created the possibility of a greater range of temporary structures than was possible in the past. It is possible to build. or buy ready made, a vast range of temporary plastic greenhouses that will fit into the smallest space. Even people who have only a balcony or terrace can now have a greenhouse.

Now that the greenhouse is no longer confined to the simpler rectangular structure it is possible to adapt them all types of space. Modern plastic materials can be cut, bent and stretched in ways that would have been impossible with glass. The change in greenhouse structure and the availability of new materials has made the greenhouse more accessible than ever before.

Know Your Greenhouse Supplies

Once your greenhouse is in place everything seems ready to go. All you have to do in put in some plants and everything will be fine. But this is not the case. You are just at the beginning of a long road of trial and error.

You can avoid some expensive mistakes by planning what kind of supplies you need. The biggest mistake is just to buy the latest and fanciest gadget you see in the catalogue. Take some time to plan what you need.

Choosing greenhouse supplies depends on what kind of greenhouse you have and what you intend to grow in it. Take time to think about what you really need.

Some supplies will only fit in a certain make or shape of greenhouse. Others will be ideal for some plants but not for others.

You should really begin this process of planning even before you choose what kind of greenhouse to buy. That way you can buy the basic essentials at the same time as you buy the greenhouse. There may be cut price deals here.

It is possible to resort to home made solutions. But if you have a beautiful redwood model you really want to keep the aesthetics in mind. A ramshackle system of plant supports may work perfectly well but will not look as good as the one your greenhouse manufacturer sells.

Decide what you are going to grow and how you are going to grow it. If you intend to plant directly into the earth you will not need benches of staging as it called. This method is often used for plants like tomatoes, squashes, cucumbers and melons where height is important.

Most greenhouses benefit from some staging. It is useful for seedlings and smaller plants. Aluminum staging is available fairly cheaply. It is durable and light if you want to move it. But it will not look good in a redwood greenhouse where you should go for staging made of timber. The whole effect will be better.

If you have an unusually shaped greenhouse, such as a solar dome, conventional staging may not fit it. In this case it is best to buy a purpose made system supplied for this kind of greenhouse.

One of the things that few people think about when they begin to use a greenhouse is shading. The purpose of a greenhouse it to maximize the heat of the sun. It seems illogical to talk about the importance of shade. But shade is vital because the sun can burn your plants.

Shading takes a variety of forms. It can be achieved by painting the glass with special paint which can be washed off in the winter. A better solution is shade netting which is clipped to the framework of the greenhouse. This is something to check with your manufacturer who may sell a system designed for your greenhouse. The same system may also be used for plant supports.

The next question is how do you intend to water your plants. You can, of course, walk out to the greenhouse with a watering can. But in the height of the growing season you would have to do this several times a day.

Most people prefer an automatic watering system. They work in different ways. Some work by feeding water through a series of drip feeds in a pipe. This method is ideal for plants in pots. Others work by spreading water through a porous hose. This method is good for plants growing in directly in the earth. You will need an outdoor water supply to set up either system in your greenhouse.

Watering systems of either type can be controlled with a timer that fits onto the water supply. It turns the fawcett on an off at the intervals you set. A system like this allows you to leave the greenhouse while you are on vacation.

An alternative is a passive watering system. This method uses capillary matting to draw water from a reservoir. A length of guttering fixed along the edge of the bench will work well. The capillary matting is draped over the edge of the bench into the water and laid under the plants. The matting must be kept covered to prevent it drying out. Gravel or black plastic can be used. So long as the reservoir is full your plants will be watered. The disadvantage of this method is that if the reservoir runs dry while you are away your plants will die.

Next to watering, ventilation is the major question in greenhouses. In the height of summer a greenhouse can become too hot. The simplest answer to this problem is to open the door. Most greenhouses come with opening vents in the roof or walls. A current of air moving through the greenhouse will keep the temperature down and deter pests such as whitefly.

Automatic systems that will open vents when the greenhouse temperature reaches a certain level are available. You may also want to consider a more elaborate solution and fit a fan. A fan may not be necessary if you are only using your greenhouse in the summer, but if you want to use it during the winter a fan is valuable. It will allow you to ventilate the greenhouse and keep heat in. The air expelled by the fan can even be recirculated by fitting a flexible hose to vent and returning it to the greenhouse.

Growing in the winter demands lighting especially in northern latitudes. Plants require lights as well as heat and moisture to grow. Some plants will only come into flower if the day length is correct. Installing lighting allows you to create an artificially long day.

But if you are not planning to grow plants in your greenhouse during the winter there is no need to have lighting. This is an area you can make savings on greenhouse supplies if you plan in advance what you intend to grow.

The same is true of heating. If you want to use you greenhouse during the winter you will need some form of heating. An electric fan heater is the best choice in most cases. Heating or lighting requires a power supply. You should think about this at an early stage. It may influence where you position your greenhouse.

Equipments You'll Need For A More Productive Greenhouse

A greenhouse is basically a very simple thing. By means of glass or plastic the sun's energy is trapped in the air and soil so that an enclosed space is warmed allowing plants to grow optimally. While the principle of the thing is very simply the devil, as they say, is in the detail.

To get the most out of your greenhouse you are going to need some supplies to make it an efficient system. Your aim is create in an artificial environment the best growing conditions for plants that would not normally thrive in northern latitudes or at high altitude. Your plants need warmth and humidity, but they also need ventilation because without a good air flow disease can result.

You also need to get the maximum number of plants into the relatively small space of your greenhouse. Whether your aim is fruit and vegetables for the kitchen or exotic flowers for the house or show bench you need to exploit your greenhouse to the full extent of its potential. Otherwise it just becomes inefficient. A greenhouse is an intensive system.

Even you rely only on the sun's rays to heat your greenhouse and do not have any form of supplementary heating you will need to think about a range of equipment. You will certainly need a method of venting the greenhouse. On a sunny day a greenhouse can become too hot and plants will suffer. The simplest method is to walk out there and open the door and a window. But if you are at work all day or plan to take vacations that is not a satisfactory solution. An automatic system of ventilation for the greenhouse is the answer.

Automatic ventilation may be as simple as an electronic mechanism that opens a window or a more elaborate system of fans. They are triggered by a thermostat. You can start with something basic and invest in a more elaborate system as you develop your greenhouse.

The same is true for watering. I could walk out to the greenhouse with a watering can. But do I want to do that four or five times a day in high season? Even the most enthusiastic grower might hesitate at that. No, an automatic watering system is the answer even for a small greenhouse. It can be quite simple. A passive system using capillary matting is cheap and easy to maintain. At a more complex level there are systems of drip feed pipes that deliver water to the plants.

For all the year round growing a greenhouse will certainly need lighting. Lights will extend your growing season. There are a number of types available for greenhouses.

Bringing power to the greenhouse is a skilled job. Get an electrician to install an outdoor power supply if you do not already have one. The control systems themselves can be built by an enthusiastic amateur. The parts are available at electronic hobbyist suppliers. Most of us would probably prefer to buy them ready made. They are a good investment in the long term because they will ensure the best conditions for your plants and allow you to take a break.

You should also think about how you intend to grow your plants. Will the plants be in containers on benches or will they grow in the ground? Plants will grow quite happily in the ground. But if you grow the same kind of plant year after year in the same place there can be a build up of disease. The traditional answer to this problem was to replace the soil in the greenhouse annually. That must have been back breaking work. A better solution is to use a growing medium that can be replaced annually. Commercial potting compost is an ideal solution. These are usually light to handle because they are based on peat or, even better, coconut fiber or bark which are both sustainable resources.

Benches, or greenhouse staging, is very useful. Smaller plants or seedlings can be placed at a higher level. They also provide space for mixing compost and repotting plants. If the greenhouse is to be used by someone who has mobility problems then this becomes even more important. A gardener with limited mobility can derive great pleasure from a greenhouse if it is planned properly. Good access is important for all gardeners but especially so for those with mobility problems. A path of well laid paving stones is essential for any greenhouse.

Supplies Needed For Your Greenhouse

Greenhouse suppliers' catalogues are full of wonderful gadgets and must-have devices for your greenhouse. But what is really essential? Let us consider what kind of supplies you really need.

At the most basic level you can get away with a watering can and plenty of time. If you can walk out to your greenhouse several times a day to water your plants and check the ventilation then you do not need to buy anything. You may need the exercise. Think of it as a health cure.

But few of us have the option to live at that pace today. We have to go to work and need to take vacations. A greenhouse has to be able to look after itself to some extent. Some degree of automation in a greenhouse is desirable, even essential.

When considering what greenhouse supplies you need an automatic watering system should be at the top of your list. Automatic watering systems work in a number of ways. The simplest is the passive system that relies on capillary matting to draw water up from a reservoir. This is the cheapest system. Alternatively you may use a piped water system that is controlled by a timer. These may feed water to individual pots through a system of drippers or spread water through a porous pipe. Alternatively, you may opt for a misting system that waters the plants and sprays fine water droplets into the air.

Ventilation can be controlled automatically too. There are electronic devices that will open a vent or the door of a greenhouse when the temperature reaches a certain level and allow them to close when the temperature drops. A more sophisticated option is to install an electric fan that will expel air from the greenhouse as the temperature rises and draw in cooler air.

It is possible to modify the extractor fan used in domestic kitchens and bathrooms or the kind that are found in cooker hoods. For those who are not able to do this a better solution is to buy a ready made one. Your greenhouse manufacturer will sell fans that fit your model of greenhouse. This is the most aesthetically satisfying solution.

Even with good watering and ventilation it will never be possible to achieve so perfect an environment for your plants that you eliminate all pests and diseases. Many gardeners opt for chemical solutions, but others prefer to use biological methods in their greenhouse. A range of predator bugs can now be bought that will deal with most common infestations in your greenhouse. The most common plant diseases in the greenhouse are related to mildew and fungus. They are caused by an inappropriate balance between temperature and humidity. If you are trying to grow plants together that require slightly different conditions it will be difficult to avoid some problems. They can be treated efficiently with a number of fungicides which tests show to be safe. But you should always use as directed and store them away from children.

Fertilizer is a vital supply for successful greenhouse growing. You must feed the plants in your greenhouse. They are growing at a tremendous rate and even if they are planted directly in the earth need nutrients.

Inorganic chemical fertilizers work well and are available in formulations that suit particular kinds of plant and particular stages of growth. You will need one fertilizer for vegetative growth and another for the flowering and fruiting stage of a plant's life.

An increasing number of gardeners prefer organic feeds for their plants. These are also widely available in liquid and powder form. They are highly effective and produce results that are just as good as the inorganic variety. The choice is yours.

Some form of shading will be necessary in most greenhouses. The heat of the sun can burn plants very easily. The best method is to clip specially made shade netting to the inside of the framework of the greenhouse. The same system of clips you use for the shade netting can be used to hold plant supports and bubble wrap plastic in the winter.

Bubble wrap is used to insulate the greenhouse. It is an optional extra. But is extremely useful and worth adding to your list of greenhouse supplies. These suggestions cover some of the supplies you will need for your greenhouse.

What Every Gardener Needs To Know About Greenhouse Systems

The greenhouse is a system that attempts to mimic the natural system in which plants grow in the wild. We must aim to provide the plants with water, light, heat and nutrients in the right quantities and at the right time for the plants to thrive. Not only that but we must aim to go one better than nature and to fine tune the greenhouse system to the point where it produces the maximum output for the minimum possible input.

The money we spend on lighting, heating and watering our greenhouse, feeding the plants and treating them for pests and diseases are the inputs. Our own time is another input and one that is often in short supply. Few of us can spend as much time as we would like in the greenhouse.

Outputs are the fruit, vegetables and flowers we harvest from our greenhouse. Somewhat less quantifiable are the physical and psychological benefits we derive from working in the greenhouse. Growing plants is a recognized way to combat stress and depression.

We want to get the most output we can from our greenhouse. Maximizing the crop is not incompatible with the personal benefits because it is a pleasure to be in a greenhouse that is working well.

It will help to think of the overall greenhouse system as a number of interconnected subsystems. When all these systems are working in harmony then the greenhouse as a whole will function effectively.

There are four basic subsystems: water, heat, light and nutrients. Let us look first at water.

Water is important because it carries nutrients to the plants' roots. It is also important to the leaves of the plant which need water to manufacture food. The atmosphere of a greenhouse needs to be moist as well as the growing medium.

Simple manual watering is often not enough when plants are in rapid growth. An automatic watering system is the ideal way of providing the correct amount of water. It can be set on a timer depending on the growing conditions and the stage of the plant's life.

The air in a greenhouse can be kept moist by misting. Automatic misting systems are available. A reservoir of water will also help.

When water is an expensive input because it is metered then rainwater should be collected. A water barrel will store water from the roof of a house and the greenhouse. It can then be pumped into the greenhouse. Small and very reliable pumps are not available for this purpose.

Heating is perhaps the most expensive input and needs to be controlled carefully by a thermostat. There is no point in having a heater on when it is not necessary. You must carefully monitor the temperature in the greenhouse and outdoors.

Insulation is good idea during the winter. This will allow you to reduce your heating bills.

Light is usually plentiful and mostly free. It only becomes an issue in the winter when the day length is short and the sky cloudy. Some artificial lighting may be necessary in a greenhouse.

The problem that light presents is that there can be too much of it. Plants easily burn in a greenhouse and shading is vital in summer.

Nutrients are vital for plant growth. You must feed the plants if you want the best results possible. The most controlled system of plant nutrition is the hydroponic system in which plant roots are suspended in a nutrient rich solution. Plants can even grow on a pane of glass if a thin film of nutrients is constantly passed over their roots. This works well in a greenhouse setting.

When all these subsystems are working well then there will be little trouble with plant diseases and pests. Where these occur it is necessary to look at heat, light, water and nutrient levels.

In theory it is possible in a large enough greenhouse to have a completely closed system with no external inputs except sunlight. The plants themselves would produce their own food and maintain the correct level of moisture. Reptiles and insects would eat pests. There would be no need for human intervention. That is not realizable on a small scale and not desirable since we want to harvest the crops our greenhouses produce.

The human element is the most important part of your greenhouse system. You are its control system. You must train yourself to do it well. As you gain experience and read about the subject you will become more proficient and your greenhouse will begin to function as an efficient system.

How Does A Greenhouse Work: The Benefits That Can Be Derived From Its Operations

When you understand how your greenhouse works you will find that you can get the most out of it. You will feel confident to experiment and try new things. Your results will be better and you will become the envy of your friends.

Whether you want to grow ornamental subject or fruit and vegetables it pays to familiarize yourself with the way a greenhouse works. Spending a little time on basic principles will pay off in the end.

A greenhouse is the first, simplest and probably still the greatest solar device known to humankind. We hear so much about solar panels and other high tech gadgets, you may even have one of those handy solar powered devices to charge batteries, but the greenhouse is in many ways a solar powered device too.

The greenhouse differs from other more recent solar powered devices in that it has been around for so long it has been refined to the point that it works really well. It does its job perfectly.

That job is heating. A greenhouse uses the sun's rays to heat up the growing medium and air in an enclosed space. It will do that without any help from us or any added extras.

In theory it would be possible to create a greenhouse that was entirely self-sufficient that could exist without any human intervention once the system was running. The plants inside it would create their own atmosphere by giving out oxygen and taking in carbon dioxide. Such a greenhouse would be a model of the entire planet.

It would have to be a very big greenhouse, certainly bigger than you would want in your backyard, and remains the stuff of science fiction at the moment. We have not quite achieved "silent running" yet. But thinking of a greenhouse in this way helps you to understand that you are dealing with a living system.

You have to play an active role to keep the living system in your greenhouse in balance. You are the control system of the greenhouse.

The greenhouse will do its job of heating as long the sun shines without any help from you. But once you put plants in there then the problems begin. The plants will not just look after themselves.

A greenhouse is too small and the plants are typically too dense for them to be self-sufficient. You will need to provide them with water and you will need to regulate the atmosphere.

When I say regulate the atmosphere what I am talking about is humidity. Humidity is the amount of water held in the air. The amount of water that air will hold depends on the temperature of the air. Air at 70 degrees will hold twice as much water as air at 55 degrees.

When the temperature of the greenhouse begins to fall the water drops out of the air. This is known as the dew point. If plants are subjected to this for a long period they are liable to suffer from various forms of rot, mold, fungus and mildew.

This is a natural part of the plant's lifecycle but not good for us if we want good quality crops from our greenhouse. You can treat the plants with chemicals. There are plenty of fungicides available on the market. But it is better to avoid the problem as far as possible by ventilating the greenhouse.

The amount of ventilation will depend on the temperature. You need more ventilation at lower temperatures. Open the door and a window, or use an extractor fan. However you do it get that air moving.

Humidity is related to watering. If you apply too much water to the growing medium or water gathers on paths and staging in the greenhouse you will have problems with humidity. Aim to have well draining paths and surfaces in your greenhouse.

It is possible to measure the humidity of your greenhouse with a sling psychrometer. This is a device consisting of two thermometers. One thermometer has a wick that can be wet. You rotate the whole device for a few minutes then take a reading from each thermometer. Subtract the reading of the wet one from the dry one and compare the reading to the chart provided. That will give you the relative humidity.

This simple device will enable you to regulate your watering and ventilation regime in the greenhouse. Once you get those right you will eliminate a lot of the problems common to greenhouses. Your greenhouse system will be working well.

The Purposes Of Hydroponics Greenhouses

Hydroponics has been practiced for centuries. It is thought that the Hanging Gardens of Babylon were a hydroponic system. In its modern form it was developed during the Second World War. US Air force personnel used hydroponics to grow crops at military bases in the Middle East and Pacific.

With the advent of new plastic materials and new growing mediums hydroponics has become a practical proposition for the amateur. It is already widely used in commercial greenhouses.

The advantage of hydroponics is that it allows the grower to control the nutrients that are fed to the plant with great exactitude. Nothing is wasted and plants get exactly the nutrients they need at each stage in their life cycle.

There are a number of methods that are suited to the amateur and can be set up in a domestic greenhouse. The most common is probably the flood and drain method but the thin nutrient film method is gaining in popularity. Both are ideally suited to the greenhouse.

An alternative method is deep water hydroponics. This is less suitable for the greenhouse. But it may have applications when used in conjunction with fish keeping. The waste excreted by the fish acts a source of nutrients for plants. This type of hydroponics or aquaculture is perhaps a little too specialized for most hobbyists but worth keeping in mind.

For most greenhouses a flood and drain system or a thin nutrient film method will work well and they are not difficult to build. The necessary supplies are available from specialist retailers most of whom have websites. They will be pleased to advise a novice about the best equipment for their greenhouse.

Many of the supplies that you will need can be sourced from your local hardware retailer. Square section rainwater guttering, plastic pipes and water tanks are easy enough to find. A great deal of a typical greenhouse hydroponic system can be made by an amateur.

The food and drain system involves flooding water into a plant container and then letting it drain out again. It is as simple as that. Your greenhouse needs to be equipped with a reservoir for water, pipes to transport it and a pump to circulate the water around the system.

You need a tray or other container with an outlet for the water. The container should be filled with a growing medium such as perlite, coconut fiber, rockwool or clay pebbles. Rockwool is most commonly used in commercial greenhouses.

The thin nutrient film works well in the greenhouse. It simply requires a water proof surface. Even a sheet of glass will do. A steady flow of water is run constantly over the roots.

Special hydroponic nutrients are available. They are designed for general use, for specific crops, or for particular stages of growth. These must be added to the reservoir in the quantity specified by the manufacturer. All the plants in your greenhouse can be fed from a common source through a system of pipes leading to and from the reservoir.

A simple hydroponic system might consist of a series of rainwater gutters running down either side of a rectangular greenhouse with a reservoir at one end. To make the most of the space in your greenhouse you can arrange the gutters in tiers. A larger greenhouse might have gutters arranged across the width of the greenhouse.

A more developed system in a large greenhouse could put the gutters on rollers so that they be moved. An efficient system of sowing at one end and harvesting at the other can be achieved using this system.

In a circular greenhouse a system of trays might be more efficient. If they all slope down to a central reservoir the need for piping will be minimized. The reservoir can be covered with decking so that you can stand on it tend the plants.

Hydroponic systems work best if the water is heated to about 55 degrees. This temperature is will be reached in most greenhouses during the summer. But in the winter you may need to heat the reservoir when you heat the rest of the greenhouse.

Hyrodoponic systems can be used out of doors, but they really come into their own in the greenhouse. The advantage of hydroponics in the greenhouse is that is allows you to exercise complete control over your greenhouse. Not only is the temperature, watering and atmosphere of the greenhouse under your hands but so is the exact level of nutrients fed to the plants.

What You Get From Lean-To Greenhouses

A lean-to greenhouse is perhaps the simplest and most versatile form of greenhouse available. It lends itself to home construction and can be fitted into a limited space. Its characteristic feature is that is makes use of an existing structure. It might be built against the wall of a house, garage or a boundary wall.

A lean-to greenhouse might be a simple temporary structure made of plastic sheeting or it might be an elaborate permanent structure that could be dignified with the name "conservatory". Either way it is a lean-to greenhouse. It differs from other types of greenhouse in not being a free-standing structure.

The lean-to greenhouse has a reputation for being a make-shift structure, but there is no reason why it should be. The classic vine house of the nineteenth century was often a lean-to structure build along the wall of the vegetable garden of an English stately home.

Those of us with smaller budgets can still take advantage of the benefits offered by a lean-to greenhouse. The main advantage that is unique to the lean-to greenhouse is that the wall against which it is built acts as a heat store. A south-facing wall that receives the sun's rays throughout the day will give out heat all night. The wall acts as a kind of storage heater. Owners of other types of greenhouse try all kinds of expedients to achieve the same kind of thermal properties that a lean-to greenhouse has naturally.

A lean-to greenhouse has greener credentials because it retains heat in this way. Less supplementary heating is needed for a lean-to greenhouse than a free standing structure. It may also offer benefits to the house that it is built against. The lean-to greenhouse can act as a source of solar heating for the house.

The other main advantage of the lean-to greenhouse is its height. Its height is limited by the height of the wall against which the lean-to greenhouse is built, but even so there is less wasted space than in many other types of greenhouse. A lean-to greenhouse offers more usable space than the popular dome shaped greenhouse.

For this reason the lean-to greenhouse is the ideal choice where space is limited. The lean-to greenhouse can even be constructed on a small patio or balcony. Even a roof garden could accommodate a lean-to greenhouse. No one need be excluded from greenhouse gardening. A comparatively small space can yield impressive results with a lean-to greenhouse.

In some cases it is possible to fill the while of a lean-to greenhouse with plants without reserving any space for an access path. The gardener can access the plants from outside the lean-to greenhouse if the sides can be opened by means of sliding panels.

As in any other greenhouse the lean-to greenhouse needs adequate provision for heating, ventilation and watering. You will probably want to automate these systems to some extent. It may be possible to achieve this more easily in a lean-to greenhouse because of its proximity to the house. With a lean-to greenhouse it is easier to run in a supply of water and electricity than it would be at some distance from the house.

Are there any disadvantages to the lean-to greenhouse? Yes, but not many and they can be overcome.

When constructing a lean-to greenhouse it is important to ensure that the a good waterproof seal is achieved with the wall. This is particularly essential if it is build against a house wall. Flashing must be used in this context. Otherwise you will get water seepage and the wall will become discolored with mould. If you are building against a garden wall this is not such a major problem.

It may be necessary to check whether your proposed lean-to greenhouse contravenes any building regulations. The size of structure or the materials may be limited. so find out before you start and make a costly mistake.

So free-standing structure or lean-to greenhouse the choice is yours. But there are many advantages to the lean-to greenhouse. The lean-to greenhouse offers the best use of space and good thermal properties. Do not let the old image of the lean-to greenhouse put you off. It is possible to develop an aesthetically pleasing design for the lean-to greenhouse.

Greenhouse Ideal For Small Areas

Many people would like to grow plants but do not have much space. You may only have a balcony or a tiny yard. The smaller the space you have the more sense it makes to use of greenhouse because it enable you to make the most of that space all the year round.

A tiny area can produce a surprising amount of plants if it is approached in the right way. You may not become self-sufficient in fruit and vegetables but you will be able to grow a supply of fresh salads and herbs or flowers for the home from even a small greenhouse.

The greenhouse is an intensive system of growing and that is what you need if you have only a small space available. Even if you have plenty of land you may want to think about a mini greenhouse next to kitchen door so that you can grab a handful of herbs or salad greens as you prepare supper. You may already have a large greenhouse but might want a small greenhouse for some extra plants.

A small greenhouse can be very simple and cheap. It may be no more than a tubular steel framework covered with a plastic tent. They usually have a zip fastener at the front so that you can open the canopy.

Greenhouses of this type are available in a range of sizes. They can be bought for under $100.

They usually have several shelves that allow you to grow a number of small plants in pots or trays. If you place it next to a south facing wall each shelf of a small greenhouse like this will receive enough life to allow the plants to thrive.

If you want to grow tall plants in your greenhouse you can take the shelves out. But there are many alternative varieties of plants that have a small form. Choose bush or tailing tomatoes, for example. They will fit happily on the shelves of your small greenhouse.

It may be an good idea to fix your greenhouse to the wall if you live in windy area or if you have children or a dog. They can easily be knocked over and your precious plants with them. If you want to use your mini greenhouse on a balcony make sure that you secure it well.

Just as in larger greenhouses it is possible to have automatic watering systems for small greenhouses. You could arrange a drip feed irrigation system that watered all your hanging baskets and planters as well as your mini greenhouse.

If all you want to do is water the mini greenhouse then a passive watering system using capillary matting may be enough. You will need a reservoir of water at the bottom. Put black plastic on each shelf and cover it with capillary matting. Soak the whole thing before you start then put the plant pots on the shelves.

You can even make a small greenhouse into a hydroponic system by putting trays on each shelf and allowing water to run down through each of them in turn. You would need a small pump. They cost less than $30. Just drill a hole in one end of each tray and tilt it slightly to allow the water to drain. Fix a pipe along the side of your mini greenhouse to take water to the top and turn on the pump.

One of the great advantages of mini greenhouses is that plants can be raised up out of the way of slugs. A whole tray of basil seedlings can be eaten by slugs before you have got out of bed in the morning. If you wrap some copper tape around the legs of your greenhouse the slugs will hesitate to climb up and get your new plants.

Plastic covered small greenhouses tend to be less long lasting that big greenhouses that are more robustly constructed. But you can get many years of use out of them. You should be prepared to change the covering on your mini greenhouse every year or so. The framework will last much longer and can be reused again and again.

If you have a very tiny space the whole mini greenhouse can be taken down in the summer and stored away until the winter. Another alternative is to take off the cover and use the shelves to display your plants. Your mini greenhouse will provide a wall of green on your balcony or patio. Take some house plants out for an airing put them on the shelves of your mini greenhouse. What would otherwise look rather utilitarian will begin to look quite decorative.

Thinking Of Buying A Greenhouse?

Due to the ever growing demand of food caused by a fast increase in human population, agrarian resources are getting over stretched. In the case of land, farmers have been tempted to increase productivity by overuse of fertilizers and elimination of pests by using chemicals. As a result, the ecological balance has been disturbed causing several problems to farmers. Furthermore, extreme weather patterns due to global warming have also raised the specter of loss of productivity. Faced with these problems, a farmer might be tempted make the difficult choice of selling off the land held by the family for years.

The solution

Scientists and agriculture experts advocate that farmers make use greenhouses. Basically, a greenhouse is an enclosed structure where crops can be grown in a controlled environment. Inside a greenhouse, conditions required for ideal growth of crops can be provided, such as water, sunlight, nutrients controlled temperature and absence of pests. Already greenhouses have been successfully used to grow flowers and tests have now shown that these can be used to increase crop productivity up to 10 times. Greenhouses can be particularly useful in increasing the productivity of fruits and vegetables.

Construction

A greenhouses can be constructed in various shapes and sizes, depending upon the climatic conditions of the area where it is to be installed. In this regard, various materials can be used in its construction. An area influenced by strong weather patterns such as winds and storms would require a metallic structure for the greenhouse to survive. The paneling of the greenhouse in these conditions would ideally require a shatter proof material, such as plastic or Plexiglas, as against common glass. Similarly, a greenhouse planned to be installed in a saline environment, exposed to a strong sea breeze for example, would require a rust proof metallic structure to ensure a reasonable service life. On the other hand, an area experiencing gentle winds and light rain could simply be made in the form of a polythene tent stretched over wood.

Usefulness

Greenhouses are especially useful during winters. Snow, frost and hails are known to cause considerable damage to crops. A greenhouse could be supplied with heaters or insulation to prevent frost during night time. Furthermore, during daytime, a greenhouse acts to trap heat from the sun within its enclosure hence the term "greenhouse effect" used to describe global warming. The "greenhouse effect" in the enclosure would provide high temperature that is needed to preserve plants during winters.

In terms of the economic aspects associated with its installation, a greenhouse is likely to pay for its installation and maintenance costs by increasing the farms profitability manifold. In this regard, a farmer must be careful so as to consider the local climatic conditions before deciding on the type of greenhouse to be installed. It would be highly recommended to consider an expert opinion before deciding to get one.

Like all other fields of business, agriculture also requires innovation and the use of research to increase its profitability. In this context, the field of agriculture also comes with its risks like other enterprises. In this case, risks take the form of diseases, pests and extreme weather patterns. A greenhouse serves to reduce these risks in order to facilitate increase in profitability. A carefully selected greenhouse would therefore lead to an increase in crop production that would ultimately contribute towards the economic uplift of the farmer.

Guidelines For Constructing Your Commercial Greenhouse

The profitability of a greenhouse greatly depends on various factors that relate to the plants that are being grown inside it. In this regard, care must be taken so as to choose the right kind of construction for the appropriate crops. Climatic conditions of the area of installation and its topography must also be given due consideration.

Types of greenhouses

There are various types of constructions available for greenhouses. These include detached greenhouses which stand independent of each other. Access can however be provided by means of a corridor linking several detached greenhouses to each other. One example of such greenhouses is the Quonset type. These are the most common type that are constructed using arched rafters and have solid walls for additional support. These are considered to be appropriate for most crops.

Another type of greenhouse is commonly known as a ridge greenhouse. These are joined through the eave by a shared gutter, thereby permitting increased productivity. Ridge type greenhouses can be either curved or gabled. While gabled greenhouses are more suitable to be covered by substantial sheets, curved greenhouses are more suited for lighter covering materials such as polytene.

Setting up a greenhouse

While planning to setup a greenhouse, several factors should be taken into account. There must be proper access to markets, utilities and transport facilities. Moreover, prospects of future expansion must also be taken into account.

Other factors that must be taken into account before setting up a greenhouse include the crops one is interested in growing, the growing season of that crop, growing period. Furthermore the growing medium such as water, soil, sand, compost must also be defined. In addition, the farming methods such as flooring, growing pots, benches etc must also be considered. Last but not the least come the financial aspects that include marketing, productivity and the investment required.

The commercial aspects

When setting up a greenhouse, there are various commercial aspects that must not be overlooked. In this respect, the area used to set up a greenhouse must be around two acres for it to be commercially viable. This requires space for vehicular traffic associated with the employed manpower as well as transport of the product. Secondly, the greenhouse must be located in an area where it is permitted by government regulations. Furthermore, there must be road access to the site to ensure efficient delivery of the harvest to the market and smooth supply of seeds, fertilizers and maintenance equipment.

It is also important that the site is located away from industrial pollution, since the product is meant for human consumption. Industrial effluents are likely to introduce poisonous chemicals into the product that would have adverse effect on peoples' health. Since a greenhouse primarily traps heat from sunlight, the site must receive ample amount of sunlight, especially during winter season.

In terms of utilities, the site must have access to water and electricity. Water is essential for the growth of all plant forms. However, the supply must be properly tested for impurities that could harm the crop. Electricity, on the other hand is essential for maintaining the controlled environment inside the greenhouse, as well as to run the equipment needed to grow and harvest the plant.

Lastly, like all other entrepreneurships, room for future expansion must be available in this case. In this regard, careful planning is the key to success. Plan well and your business will flourish.

5 Essentials For A Commercial Greenhouse

The demand for commercial greenhouses has experienced a rapid increase in the United States. The state of Georgia alone accounts for over 11 million square feet area covered with commercial greenhouses. This sprout can well be attributed to rise in the demand for natural food products. While commercial greenhouses do provide an excellent opportunity to farmers for increasing the productivity and profitability of their holdings, it must be borne in mind that provision of essential equipment is critical for realizing these benefits. In this regard, a commercial greenhouse must be equipped with the following essentials:

1. Commercial greenhouse heaters

During the winter season, at times the provision of a heat source inside a greenhouse may be critical to ensure crop survival. Even one cold day could significantly reduce the productivity plants. Since a greenhouse normally traps heat from sunlight within its enclosure, a heater might come in handy during cloudy days. It is therefore advisable to install a reliable commercial heater in a commercial greenhouse. The cost of running the heater during sunless days would definitely be outweighed by the increase in productivity.

2. A durable greenhouse staging

A commercial greenhouse is more likely to witness heavier loads being places and transported within its compound than non-commercial greenhouses. These include greater loads of harvest, heavy pots and benches that are used to grow the plants. It is therefore important that the greenhouse staging used to move these heavy loads within the greenhouse is heavy duty and durable.

3. Seed tray shelf

Most commercial crops germinate from seeds and in order to cultivate maximum number of crops through out the year, one must ensure the provision of seed tray shelves or racks. Since space is precious inside a greenhouse, these racks or shelves could spare room that could be used to grow additional crops. In this way productivity can be further increased.

4. Watering equipment

Commercial greenhouses are by definition much more extensive that their non-commercial counterparts. It is therefore tiresome and too demanding to water the crops manually. Furthermore, keeping a track of the plants that have been watered is also quite a challenge if manual watering is undertaken. An modern and efficient plant watering system is therefore essential in a commercial greenhouse to ensure optimal productivity during harvest.

5. Thermometers

The basic purpose of a greenhouse is to provide plants with optimal ambient conditions that would lead to maximum productivity. Of these, temperature is most critical. It is therefore not advisable to rely solely on human instincts to control this vital parameter. In this context, it is important to note that even slight variations in temperature could greatly affect the amount of harvest that you reap. Moreover, its is too tiresome for a person to monitor the temperature inside the greenhouse round the clock. The provision of thermometers must therefore be ensured in a commercial greenhouse. In this regard, an automatic temperature control mechanism which does not require a human operator would be preferable.

The provision of these essential gadgets would considerably increase the productivity of a greenhouse. That would in turn boost profits that are the spirit behind any commercial enterprise. Furthermore, successful commercial farmers can rightly take pride in the contribution they make for the benefit of the community, the environment and even the whole of humanity.

Commercial Greenhouse Kits

Commercial greenhouse kits could prove to be quite useful for new entrants into this project. It provides the investor with the right kind of tools and equipment needed to undertake this business. With such a kit, one can immediately embark upon a commercial greenhouse project.

Points to be considered before purchasing commercial greenhouse kits

Before actually making the purchase, you must plan well, get your course straight and be mindful of your targets. It is therefore strongly advised that you do proper pre-purchase planning and research, and ponder over the various pros and cons associated with your project. In this context, it would be worthwhile that you gather maximum information about greenhouses.

Secondly, before going for the purchase, one must decide on the size of greenhouse That would be set up. This depends upon the size of one's holding and the nature of the crop and the amount investment that is available. Indeed, an oversized greenhouse will be more expensive to maintain if you do not have enough capital to fully populate it with plants. Empty spaces might still be using up your resources and could add to your overheads.

Another important point that must be considered before acquiring your kit is the type of plants that would fill up your greenhouse. Since, a commercial venture is always valued in terms of profitability, it is advisable to grow crops that are in demand. Once the type of crop is decided, the parameters associated with the greenhouse, such as its size, the medium of cultivation and the environment that is to be maintained inside can be determined. Incase your crops require more space, your kit should include space saving equipment such as racks. In case the plants are sensitive to temperature variation, it is a good idea to get a kit that includes sensitive thermometers and temperature control gadgets such as heaters and thermostat based mechanisms to regulate temperature.

There are various types of commercial greenhouse that are available. Choosing the best design that is ideal for your business is also an important decision you need to make before you actually go on to purchase a commercial greenhouse kit. In this regard, you must be mindful of your requirements it terms of the topography and climate of your site. Going for an expensive design that may not be required in your area could unnecessarily drain your budget. The amount wasted thus could alternatively be used to buy other useful equipments that could increase the size of your harvest.

Footnote: When buying a commercial greenhouse kit, you must be clear about your requirements in order to buy the right stuff to start your business.

Free Greenhouse Plan For You

"Plant lovers", that is people who have a passion towards maintaining gardens in their backyards and tending to plants would naturally be interested in erecting a greenhouse. In this context, a greenhouse should be well designed and constructed so that it is easy to maintain and does not give trouble to its owner.

In order to ensure the well being of plants grown inside it, a greenhouse must have an efficient watering and misting propagation system. Such a system should monitor and maintain the level of humidity within the greenhouse. Water is a precious natural resource that should be conserved. Remember, one of the benefits ascribed to greenhouses is that they are good for the environment. Your greenhouse must be able to make use of rainwater, instead of relying solely in water being supplied as a utility. A system of gutters and downspouts must therefore be in place to water the crop using natural rainwater. It would also be a good idea to have a provision for storing rainwater for future usage.

The greenhouse must be provided with electricity or natural gas (whichever is convenient) to fuel heaters that would be useful in maintaining optimal temperature during cold spells. It may be taken into account that plants utilize light to grow by the process of photosynthesis. Lights may therefore be installed inside so that plant growth is not stunted due to lack of sunlight.

Over the internet, one can find many websites that offer guidelines on how to setup a greenhouse. These may include plans that would offer help in planning the greenhouses with water supply systems. Others may contain instructions on how to get acquainted with and apply the currently popular techniques of hydroponics gardening. Some websites also offer free plans for setting up a freestanding greenhouse.

Constructing your greenhouse

For beginners, The following guidelines would be helpful in setting up a small greenhouse using low-cost, easy to acquire materials:

For setting up your greenhouse you would need items including about one and a half dozen squeeze clips, a roll of duct tape, 3 rolls heavy duty 3M clear tape, 6 mm clear plastic, 18 ratcheting tie downs, 4 to 8 T posts, 10 x 20 Universal canopy and optional lights and heaters. While assembling the greenhouse, it would be convenient to seek assistance of 2-3 persons who may be your friends or family members. These people could give you a helping hand in setting up the framework and holding things in position while you install them. While making connections, duct tape must be used properly so as to ensure that connection points are leak-proof.

First, you must connect the 18 tie-downs to connect to the upper part of the frame. You may use four T posts to support the four corners of the structure. Once this is done, place an extra T-post inside the frame and drill it at least 12" into the ground. In the next step, use the plastic sheet to cover your greenhouse. Stretch the sheet over framework that has already been installed, using a ladder. Use some heavy objects like stones, piles of gravel or even flowerpots so that the sheet remains firmly on the ground and does not blow away by wing.

Congratulations! You have made your very own low-cost greenhouse.

Greenhouse Accessories And Their Utility

A greenhouse is designed to incubate plants within its enclosure in order to protect them from climatic extremities in terms of temperature, humidity and wind. Its functions on the basis of the "greenhouse effect" whereby sunlight and infra red radiation from the sun enters the greenhouse. Upon reflection, these rays are trapped inside greenhouse, thereby contributing to a rise in temperature within it. It is worth observing the fact that in this simple setup, the source of heat is primarily the sun. However, during time periods when sunlight is not available due to cloudy skies, heaters may be employed to maintain optimum temperature. Alternately, during hot spells, temperature may be brought down by means of mist sprayers or exhaust fans.

Since maintenance of suitable conditions within its extent is the primary function of a greenhouse, certain gadgets are deemed essential for its proper exploitation. The use of these gadgets is necessary to maintain the conditions within the greenhouse at the level necessary for plant survival. These accessories include:

Thermometers

Temperature is the most critical parameter that must be regulated within a greenhouse to ensure a healthy plantation. Very cold temperatures are likely to stunt the growth of plants and in certain cases may lead to their destruction. Hot conditions, on the other hand, could "burn out" the plants. By means of thermometers, the temperature inside a greenhouse can easily be monitored and remedial measures can be planned whenever it goes critical.

Thermostats

Thermostats are automatic devices that are able to not only detect temperature changes, but can also regulate it. These could be in the form of a simple automated window that opens to the atmosphere in case temperature levels go extreme. Other more sophisticated thermostats can also be installed to maintain temperature levels in a greenhouse.

Humidistat

Maintenance of humidity within a greenhouse is also important for the well being of plants. AS in the case of a thermostat which regulates temperature, humidistats are devices that maintain moisture levels to optimum inside a greenhouse. These devices are particularly useful during hot conditions, when moisture contents available to plants are depleted by atmospheric heat causing them to dehydrate and burn. Once plants get "burnt", they essentially lose chlorophyll - the substance that gives them their green color. Chlorophyll is essential for the process of photosynthesis by which plants manufacture nutrients.

Lighting systems

Plants manufacture their food using nutrients from the soil, moisture and sunlight. This process is known as photosynthesis whereby energy from sunlight is
used to power the chemical reaction that produces carbohydrates in the presence of chlorophyll. Carbohydrates are the basic units that make up our food.
During certain climatic spells when sunlight is not available for prolonged time periods, gadgets known as grow lights can provide a useful alternative,
thereby preventing degeneration of crops.

Light meters

Like all other recourses, too much of light may be harmful for plant health. This recourse, like temperature and water, must also be provided at optimum level. Light meters can assist in detecting the amount of light plants are being exposed to inside the greenhouse. Subsequently, light can be regulated by using simple light filters like frosted glass.

While planning to install the aforementioned accessories, one must be mindful of the local conditions prevailing in the area where the greenhouse is situated. It is primarily these conditions which dictate the type of accessory to be installed in the greenhouse.

Greenhouse Designs

Given the vast number of benefits associated with them, in terms of plant health, environment as well as profitability, greenhouses are certainly worth the investment made to install and maintain them. This is true for both amateur gardeners as well as seasoned horticulturalists. For hobbyists, the amount of joy one gets from seeing their plants bloom is enough to repay their investment. For professional investors, the financial gains associated with a greenhouse are plentiful. However, since purchasing your greenhouse can be expensive owing to profits and commissions associated with those involved in its manufacturing, transportation, marketing and sale, it is important that you choose the design that is best suited to your needs, as well as installable in at your site.

Types of greenhouses

Basically greenhouses can be classified into two broad categories: the attached type and the freestanding type.

Freestanding greenhouses

Greenhouses that fall in this category can be distinguished for the other type in that these are freestanding structures erected independent of your house. As a result, these type of greenhouses can be situated so as to receive maximum exposure to sunlight. However, since it is separate from the house, the greenhouse needs to be equipped with lighting and should be supplied with electricity and water. This category can further be subdivided into two classes:

1. Juliana greenhouse

Structures conforming to this category are best suited for limited spaces. This design is also suited for first timers. Since neither silicone nor clips are used in its construction, it creates the impression of a fresh design.

2. *Hideaway design*

This design is marked by its spaciousness. It can also serve as a getaway from everyday routines where you can relax alone. Since this design employs see-through polycarbonate material. This material comes coated with an ultraviolet coating. Ultraviolet rays from sunlight are particularly harmful to humans as they can cause sunburns and skin cancer. These rays are also not good for plants. Since this type of greenhouse is designed such that it filters the carcinogenic ultra-violet light, the resulting soft dispersed light is good for your health as well as your plants. In this way you can also bask in sun without having to worry about sunburns and skin cancer. The absence of the harmful UV rays also means that you do not have to periodically apply sun blocks to protect yourself.

Attached greenhouses

Attached greenhouses are not free standing structures, but rely on your house for their structural support and integrity. Examples of this type include the even-span type and the window mounted type. The former design can be classified as a full-size model, except that one of its side is attached to the house for support. It provides more space to plants that a window-mounted design. The window mounted design, on the other hand, is fastened in a window. This type is very economical and requires least amount of space.

While prices vary depending on the design you choose, it is important that you choose the right design that suites your needs. Even an inappropriate design comes with its cost and if you are not satisfied with it, it would be a waste of time as well as money.

Fertilizing Greenhouse Plants

Green plants are characterized by their ability to manufacture their own food by a process called photosynthesis. By this process, plants combine carbon dioxide from air, and water and nutrients from the soil, like nitrates, phosphates and sulfates, to make food substances. Sunlight is used as the source of energy to power this process. While the simplest food product is in the form of carbohydrates, which only formed from carbon dioxide and water, higher organic compounds like proteins and minerals that are essential parts of growth need nutrients from soil. Fertilizers act as a source for these nutrients. Fertilizers also add porosity to the soil, which is important in the sense that it increases the soil's capacity to hold water and air without drowning the plant.

Fertilizers could be in solid form or liquid. The type of fertilizer needed for your crops depends on the type of plants you have planted. This is due to the fact that each plant has its own needs for different substances that are essential for its growth. During seasons that stimulate rapid growth of certain plants, like in the spring season, these plants must be fertilized once a month or two. Plants that experience continuous growth throughout the year, on the other hand, require a steady supply of fertilizers.

What are fertilizers?

As mentioned before, fertilizers are substances that act as sources of essential nutrients like nitrogen, iron, phosphorous, sulfur and other elements. Nitrogen is the most important of these since it is used to make proteins. Proteins are one of the main food groups along with fats and carbohydrates. Unlike fats and carbohydrates, which only contain carbon, hydrogen and oxygen, proteins contain nitrogen in addition to these three elements. Proteins are regarded as building blocks of life. In order to supply this essential element, fertilizers are rich in nitrogen, which is usually around 50%. Peat-like fertilizers, which contain nitrate-F are preferable for use in greenhouses by hobbyists. Greenhouse Gradecalcium nitrate in could also be applied for large scale growing.

Application of fertilizers

Fertilizers are usually recommended for certain types of plants. Before applying to your plants, you must carefully read the label and seek an expert opinion regarding their use. Suppliers and catalogues can also give you useful information regarding their use. The opinion of a qualified agriculturalist of a plant pathologist would certainly be more useful.

It is important that fertilizers supply a balanced diet to plants for their growth. Soluble or liquid fertilizers deliver quicker results as compared with solid ones. Their application is as simple as watering plants. Stronger than recommended doses are however not recommended as these would injure their roots and could eventually kill them. It is therefore a good idea to actually apply weaker than recommended doses to plants. This ca easily be done by diluting the fertilized with water.

Applying a mixture of different grades of fertilizers is also a good technique so as to fulfill the needs of the type of plants that are being cultivated. This will also ensure that the plant is supplied with the specific chemicals it needs at the various stages of its life.

Greenhouse plants need your attention. Checking them each day for their well being is both satisfying and give you a sense of accomplishment. Be sure that they are free from disease and pests and flourish. Their survival is your success.

Fertilization Of Greenhouse Crops

Greenhouses are used to provide crops with a favorable environment that would trigger their healthy growth. While the provision of optimal temperature, humidity level and water supply are primary concerns in a greenhouse, the supply of nutrients is also an important aspect that must be catered for in a greenhouse.

What are fertilizers?

Plants are able to manufacture their own food by a process called photosynthesis. By this process, plants combine carbon dioxide from air, and water and nutrients from the soil, like nitrates, phosphates and sulfates, to make food substances. Sunlight is used as the source of energy to power this process. While the simplest food product is in the form of carbohydrates, which only formed from carbon dioxide and water, higher organic compounds like proteins and minerals that are essential parts of growth need nutrients from soil. Fertilizers act as a source for these nutrients. Fertilizers also add porosity to the soil, which is important in the sense that it increases the soil's capacity to hold water and air without drowning the plant. In open nature, plants receive a constant supply of nutrients in the form of decaying organic matter and animal waste in the form of manure. However, since a greenhouse is secluded from the open environment, the supply of nutrients is essential. Fertilizers are essentially substances that act as sources of essential nutrients like nitrogen, iron, phosphorous, sulfur and other elements. Nitrogen is the most important of these since it is used to make proteins. Proteins are one of the main food groups along with fats and carbohydrates. Unlike fats and carbohydrates, which only contain carbon, hydrogen and oxygen, proteins contain nitrogen in addition to these three elements. Proteins are regarded as building blocks of life. In order to supply this essential element, fertilizers are rich in nitrogen.

Types of fertilizer

Fertilizers could be in solid form or liquid. The type of fertilizer needed for your crops depends on the type of plants you have planted. This is due to the fact that each plant has its own needs for different substances that are essential for its growth. The Specific nutrients contained in a fertilizer also determine its category.

Nutrient contents

Since different elements are needed for healthy growth of plants, fertilizers are rich in them. These elements include:

1. Nitrogen

Nitrogen is the most important of these since it is used to make proteins. Proteins are one of the main food groups along with fats and carbohydrates. Unlike fats and carbohydrates, which only contain carbon, hydrogen and oxygen, proteins contain nitrogen in addition to these three elements. Proteins are regarded as building blocks of life. In order to supply this essential element, fertilizers are rich in nitrogen, which is usually around 50%. This essentially takes the form of nitrate compounds.

2. Potassium

The most common source of this essential element in fertilizers is potassium nitrate. Potassium is needed by the plant for proper utilization of water.

3. Phosphorus

This element is a must for plant growth. While it is usually supplied in large amounts, over dosage could hamper the solubility of other nutrients needed by plants. Phosphorus is usually added in the form of super phosphate or phosphoric acid.

In addition to the aforementioned, other nutrients like iron, magnesium, sulfur, zinc, copper, calcium, potassium, chloride etc are also required. These could be supplied either through the growth medium, or by supplemental application.

The amount of the nutrients being supplied must be carefully monitored. Only by proper application can optimum plant growth be reached which would ultimately lead to a good harvest and high profits.

Heating Up A Greenhouse

Certain geographical locations experience climatic extremes in terms of temperature. In these conditions, many plant species are unable to survive, prompting farmers to practice crop rotation. As a result, crops appear in the market during specific seasons. Since there is demand for cash crops throughout the year, large amounts of crops have to be imported and transported from other climatic locations, leading to rise in prices during offseason. However, to overcome this problem, researchers have come up with the idea of growing them in greenhouses equipped with heaters. Nevertheless, heaters are expensive devices and one must choose the best option available, depending upon the type of crop, the specific requirements of the crop and the weather conditions of the locality.

Greenhouse heaters typically use 1.8-4.8 Watts of energy, depending upon the volume of air being heated inside the greenhouse. For larger sized greenhouses, several heaters may be needed. However, the higher price during off seasons is likely to offset their running cost. Moreover, these products would certainly compete well against imported ones, since they are likely to be fresh products than their imported counter parts, which usually travel long distances to reach the market.

Types of greenhouse heaters

There are various types of greenhouse heaters that are suitable for greenhouse. They are mostly classified based on the type of fuel they consume. While purchasing a heater, you must be sure there is ready access to the type of input your selected heater requires. Based on the criterion of fuel type, the various options available include:

1. Electric heaters

These heaters are best suited for amateur hobbyists since they do not discharge effluents and are sake to use even when left unmonitored during night time. Furthermore, they are not bulky, and an be installed on the ground or can suspended from the ceiling.

2. Gas heaters

These heaters are fueled by natural gas propane. Since flue gas is produced from them, proper ventilation is required for complete combustion. Without proper ventilation, their use can be dangerous since incomplete combustion produces carbon monoxide, which is poisonous for both humans as well as plants. These heaters can be costly if you do not have a cheap source of natural gas in your greenhouse.

3. Paraffin heaters

As in the case of gas heaters, paraffin heaters emit smoke and thus require a smoke stack. They also require a reliable source of fuel for their operation to be economical.

4. Coal heaters

Similar to other non-renewable fuel heaters, these heaters require a reliable supply of coal to continue operation, as well as proper ventilation for air supply as well as expulsion of flue gases.

Important consideration

For a heater to be effective, the greenhouse must be properly insulated for the heat to remain inside its enclosure. While 100% insulation is impossible, efforts must be made to minimize heat loss, otherwise the cost of fuel is likely to erode the profitability of your venture. For best results, the expert advise must be sought in order to acquire the most suitable heater for your greenhouse. Since it is a major investment, proper homework must be done before making the purchase.

Maintaining Humidity Levels Inside A Greenhouse

Plants require water as well as sunlight and carbon dioxide to manufacture their food. This is accomplished through a process called photosynthesis. With out the presence of the three aforementioned agents, photosynthesis seizes to occur. As a result the plant starves and dies. While it is important to water plants regularly, it is also essential to maintain the optimum level of humidity in the atmosphere for the plants' well being. The importance of humidity can be gauged through an understanding of the process of transpiration.

Transpiration

Plants absorb water from their roots. This water is transported by the process of osmosis to specialized tissues, known as xylem, which specialize in transporting water all the way up to the leaves. It is essentially in the leaves that the process of photosynthesis takes place. In addition to water, the essential nutrients needed by plants are also carried to the leaves, dissolved in water. From the leaves, excess water is released into the atmosphere in the form of water vapors. The evaporation of water plays an important part in keeping the plants cool. It also serves to transport nutrients up to the leaves, since in the absence of evaporation, leaves would get water logged, whereby the xylem tissues will get saturated and no further absorption of water will be possible by the roots. This process of transporting water from the roots to the leaves and its subsequent release into the atmosphere is called transpiration.

For the process of transpiration to occur smoothly, the level of humidity in air must be at an optimum level. In case there is excess humidity, water will not evaporate in leaves, thereby creating a condition where leaves get over soaked. As a result, the supply of nutrients to the leaves gets halted. On the contrary, if the level of humidity drops below normal, excessive evaporation will occur, saturating the leaves with nutrient salts, as well as depleting water level in the soil. A fully grown tree may lose several hundred liters of water through its leaves in hot and dry conditions. About 90% of the water that is absorbed by the plant's roots is used up in this process. In the absence of water, plant will be unable to synthesize their food and will starve. Furthermore, excessive transpiration will also drop their temperature below normal.

Maintaining humidity inside the greenhouse

Evaporative coolers can help in maintaining temperature as well as humidity inside a greenhouse. Other units are available that package warmers and humidifiers to maintain temperature and humidity. Humidifiers can effectively control moisture level in air. Other gadgets that accompany humidifiers are directional airflow louvers, which maintain flow of air, thereby humidifying, ventilating, and cooling the ambience inside the greenhouse.

Coolers available commercially are designed to suite their purpose in a greenhouse. Some models have heavy-gauge, zinc-coated metallic louvers and cabinets featuring zinc-chromate.

The amount of sunlight received by plants depends on seasonal climatic conditions. Over exposure to the sun can occur during summers. It is advisable to install cooling and humidifying systems so as to maintain the right temperature in the greenhouse. This utility extends during the winter season, when sunlight could be scarce.

Proper heating and ventilation in a greenhouse is important to grow healthy plants and appropriate systems must be installed to maintain temperature and humidity at optimal levels.

<u>5 Factors To Consider When Choosing Greenhouse Lighting</u>

In simple terms, a greenhouse is meant to grow plants in a controlled environment that provides them with optimal conditions needed for their well being. This essentially means that plants are no longer growing in open nature, but inside secured enclosures. The individual responsible for the greenhouse must therefore ensure that plants are provided with suitable conditions similar to the ones enjoyed by their counterparts growing in nature.

Light

Plants manufacture their food by the process of photosynthesis. In nature, this process consumes sunlight, water and carbon dioxide to manufacture carbohydrates and other organic compounds that serve a food and are essential for the growth of plants. It is therefore important that plants receive adequate sunlight inside the greenhouse. This is especially the case in winters, when sunlight is scarce. It is here that utility of artificial lights comes into play. Various different types or artificial lighting systems are available in the market today. Selecting a suitable lighting system can nonetheless prove tricky, especially for those unfamiliar with them.

Factors to be considered when purchasing greenhouse lighting

Before actually buying a greenhouse lighting system, you must bear in mind the following considerations so as to get the most suitable light for your hothouse.

1. Type of your greenhouse

Before selecting the light, you must consider the type of greenhouse you are going to install it in. Whether it is a commercial or a personal greenhouse. The type of greenhouse dictates the type of light that is most suited to it. For a commercial greenhouse, the lighting system must be able to bear adverse operating conditions that are usually found inside.

2. Operating hours

The amount of light usage in the greenhouses is based on "photoperiods." Photoperiods are defined as time intervals during which light will be switched on. The duration of these photoperiods varies, depending upon the season, climate and location of the greenhouse. A photoperiod of 12 hours means that in 24 hours of a day, lights will only be operating for 12 hours.

It is therefore important that the light purchased will be able to operate for time periods that are equal to the required photoperiods.

3. Purpose

You must purchase a lighting system that will focus on your requirements. In case you want to induce growth in flowering plants, it is best to buy a source that will emit more "spectrum colors" like red, blue and the "far-red wavelengths." The colors contained in the light being emitted have considerable effect on growth of plants. This means that not all colors in the light spectrum produce the required effects.

4. Electrical efficiency

Lighting systems are almost always powered by electricity. This means that operating a lighting system will add to your electricity bills. Electrical efficiency can play an important part in reducing your bills, while proving the same amount of luminosity.

5. Heat

No light source is 100% efficient. This means that some amount of electrical input will always be converted into heat that will be emitted by the light source. In so many words, a light that is more a heater than a light is no good. Overheating could actually kill your plants.

Lighting is a very important parameter that contributes towards the development of a plant. It is therefore important to buy the lighting system that is best suited for your greenhouse so as to ensure healthy growth of your plants.

The Business Relationship Between Farmers And Greenhouse Manufacturers

Ever since farming evolved eons ago, man has appreciated the importance of irrigation and sunlight for harvesting good crops. Alongside, since ancient times problems posed by bad weather, plant diseases and pests have also existed. As a result, scientists and farmers have developed fertilizers, pesticides and herbicides to ensure a successful crop.

While initially, the use of artificial fertilizers and chemical pesticide and herbicide did show improved yields, in the longer run their harmful effects started to raise problems. As a result, farmers and scientist propose to go revert to organic farming practices.

The benefits of greenhouses

Greenhouse offer a solution for protecting crops against the adverse climate and pests, by providing a closed environment where plants can grow throughout the year without being attacked by pests and plant diseases.

Construction of a greenhouse

Greenhouses are usually constructed using a wooden or metallic framework over which glass panels are laid to isolate the interior from the outside environment. However this simple structure may not be enough to withstand adverse weather, pests and plant diseases, as well as degradation of the structure itself. Manufacturers have therefore come up with innovative models using new materials.

Greenhouse frames can now be fabricated from aluminum or plastic members, which are rust as well as termite resistant. Panels used to cover structure can alternatively be made of plastic or film. These materials are shatter proof as against glass and thus able to withstand heavy snow and hail storms. Furthermore, these materials are scratch proof and can sustain impact from even from a rock is hurled at the panel. Furthermore, as compared with glass, these materials are known offer better protection against ultraviolet rays from the sun. Ultraviolet or UV rays are well known cancer agents and are harmful to both plants and humans. The construction of a greenhouse ultimately depends on the requirements of the cultivator and the area available for the purpose.

The role of greenhouse manufacturers

Greenhouse manufacturers, in addition to making shelters for the plants, also provide instruments and gadgets That help in maintaining a favorable environment needed to sustain plant growth. Farmers who cultivate crops in cold regions require heaters that would keep plants warm during cold spells. Manufacturers can also supply timers that supply water intermittently during the day so that plants can absorb water and nutrients that are needed for proper growth.

Manufacturers who have done business over years can offer useful advice with regards to installation, and commissioning of the greenhouse, the proper equipment it needs to be equipped with. They can also acquaint the farmer with innovative farming techniques like hydroponics.
Using water as the growth medium instead of soil, this technique is known to prevent plant diseases and pests, thereby increasing productivity by 4-6 times.

Many manufacturers also offer to install and commission the greenhouse within warranty. This is offer particularly useful since greenhouses are heavy and contain items that are delicate to handle. Damaged equipment is usually costly for the farmer to replace.

Working together with greenhouse manufacturers would enable farmers to enhance their yields thus increasing their profits. Furthermore, fruits, vegetables and flowers would be available in the market all the year round.

Identifying The Best Greenhouse Manufacturer

Most people are brand conscious when it comes to buying a product. The brand actually gives an idea about the quality of that particular product. Manufacturers in turn endeavor to maintain the quality of that standard since they stand to lose their market if they compromise the quality.

Like other products you must consider the manufacturer and the brand when you buy a greenhouse. Most of the greenhouses available can be bought off the shelf in the form of kits. Others are available in assembled form or specially constructed models. It is important that you are sure of the quality of components that are used in making the greenhouse.

While considering different manufacturers, one must bear the following points in mind to strike a good deal.

1. Do your homework

before going for the purchase, you must identify your specific requirements that pertain to the area you plan to install your hot house in, and the type of plants you are looking forward to cultivate. A brand known to produce good results in some area or for a certain kind of crop may not be suitable in your location or for your crops. It is therefore advisable seek advice from people who are already engaged in greenhouse businesses.

2. Know the manufacturer

After identifying a suitable greenhouse for your self, The best thing to do is to check on its manufacturer. A seemingly flashy product does not automatically guarantee good quality. Such a check can often certify the quality of the greenhouse you have chosen. A good manufacturer usually guarantees customer satisfaction. As a result, you automatically get insured against malfunctions and quality related defects.

3. Certifications

It is wise to check with the manufacturer if it is affiliated with a reputed association. If you buy a greenhouse from a manufacturer affiliated with such a body, you would be sure that dealing with a reliable company.

Furthermore, you should make sure you buy your hothouse from a manufacturer who implements international quality and ,material standards such as the ISO 9000 and ASTM standards while making the product.

4. Look around

Going outright for the first manufacturer that you come across is never recommended, even it is a highly reputable company. It is better to look around for more. This way you will get a chance to carry out a market survey that will enable you interact with different manufacturers or their agents, compare prices of different brands and parts and identify different options that are commercially available.

The best bargain may not depend entirely on the repute and expertise of the manufacturer. The price paid for the product is also a major factor in getting a fair deal. Furthermore, most new entrants in the market offer products that are quality certified and comparable to existing market leaders at a cheaper price.

5. The internet

On the internet, one gets a huge variety of brands to evaluate and choose from. If there are not many vendors in your vicinity or you cant afford the time to actually carry out a physical market survey, then internet is the answer. Over the internet, you get to evaluate the brand without much difficulty. Furthermore, an online survey also has the advantage of accessing reviews provided by consumers themselves.

Selecting the most suitable greenhouse manufacturer can prove to be very laborious. However, at the end of the day you get the benefit of it in terms your personal satisfaction.

Paneling Up The Greenhouse

Across the globe, ever since the advent of civilization, man has cultivated crops in the open environment. Even today, most of the plantations stand in open air. However, in the open environment, forces of nature can not be controlled. This is the reason why some farmers opt for greenhouses where conditions can be effectively monitored to suit the plants' needs.

The greenhouse is a combination of a frame with panels installed over it. The frame provides the basic structure of the greenhouse while panels form the roof and walls of greenhouse. Panels are designed let in sunlight so as to keep the plants warm for maximum growth. They do this by trapping the heat from the sun within itself. If the plants inside do not require a lot of sunlight, panels can be covered with opaque covers to block excess sunlight from entering the enclosure.

In the past, greenhouse panels were made from glass. Since glass is not shatter proof, it is vulnerable during hailstorms and heavy snowfall. Nowadays, alternate materials such a acrylic or plastic are available, which are shatterproof.

Types of panels available in the market

There are three types of panels readily available in the market.

1. Glass

The most common material used to make greenhouse panels is glass. Ordinary glass does not provide protection against ultraviolet rays from the sun, excessive exposure to which can be detrimental to plants. Furthermore, since ordinary glass is prone to shatter, tempered glass which is stronger than regular glass is often used as an alternate. A reputable contractor must be hired to install glass panels because of their weight and fragility.

2. Plastic

Plastic panels can be made from fiberglass, polyester, acrylic or polycarbonate. These materials can withstand impact from hails, heavy snowfall, balls and rocks. In addition, plastic panels are lightweight and allow optimum amount of sunlight to enter the greenhouse.

3. Film panels

This type uses a film that is stretched over the panel. Usually polyethylene and polyester films are used in greenhouse panels. These panels offer adequate protection from the sun. Moreover, these panels are economical and can be purchased in the form of rolls.

Choosing the panel most suitable for you

Each of the aforementioned panels comes with its advantages and disadvantages. Choosing the right type will depends on the usage of the greenhouse and the kinds of plants that would be cultivated within. Having the most suitable panels will ensure that plants would be able to grow round the year.

Panels can either be purchased from the vendor or be custom made to fit the greenhouse. Both cultivator and the contractor should measure the site before the panels are made so as to ensure proper size. If hiring a contractor is beyond the farmer's budget, certain websites on the internet that offer services at a lower price could be explored.

Plants manufacture their food by the process of photosynthesis. In nature, this process consumes sunlight, water and carbon dioxide to manufacture carbohydrates and other organic compounds that serve a food and are essential for the growth of plants. It is therefore important that plants receive adequate sunlight inside the greenhouse. This is especially the case in winters, when sunlight is scarce. It is therefore important that the right kind of panels are installed, which will allow ample amount of light to reach plants, while protecting them against the harmful ultraviolet radiation present in sun rays.

Choosing And Comparing Greenhouse Panels

Panels form the walls and ceiling of your greenhouse. In order to enable the hothouse to actually be able to retain heat within its confines, these panels must be able to insulate its enclosure from the outside surroundings. In this way, heating costs can be kept within reasonable limits.

Individuals seeking to install a greenhouse as a hobby, must consider the properties of the panel material and check whether it conforms with the needs of the plants that are to be cultivated in the greenhouse. It is also advisable to go for an insulative and fireproof panel.

Various materials are available for greenhouse panels, with each material having its pros and cons. Glass, fiberglass, and polycarbonates, are better suited for a greenhouse hobbyist. Plastic panels, on the other hand are more popular with commercial greenhouses operators. Plastic panels, however, are not particularly durable and require frequent replacement.

Glass panels

Glass paneling very attractive in appearance. They are also easy to maintain since they are less vulnerable to scratches. They also have a long life unless subjected to impact that could shatter the glass. Glass paneling is a good choice from aesthetic point of view. In addition to giving your greenhouse a pleasant outlook, glass panels transmit large amounts of light into the greenhouse.

The density of glass, on the other hand, is quite high as compared with other panel materials. In case glass panels are selected, the foundation and framing must be strong enough to sustain its weight. Moreover, since glass is fragile as well as heavy, it is quite expensive to install glass panels. In this regard, professional assistance must be sought and care must be taken so as to prevent personal injury as well as material damage.

Polycarbonate

While polycarbonate panels are not as appealing as their glass counterparts, they are more durable. Furthermore, their insulative properties are also quite good, especially when used in a double or triple sheet configuration. This enables the greenhouse to contain more heat within, thereby reducing heating costs. However, compared with glass, polycarbonate lacks transparency. As a result, sunlight let in through these panels is not as intense as in the case with glass.

Fiberglass

Panels made from fiberglass are strong, lightweight and shatter-proof. However, a good quality fiberglass must be selected for the panels as a poor grade is likely to discolor, thus reducing light penetration with time.

The resin coating present in the case of fiberglass eventually wears off, causing dirt to accumulate between the fibers. Therefore, a new resin coating must be applied after about 15 years. While initially the transparency is comparable with that of glass, it reduces with time, especially in the case of poor quality fiberglass.

Plastic panels

Both polycarbonate or acrylic plastic, have heat-saving as well as long-life attributes. While acrylic does not discolor, polycarbonate usually turns yellow. Both materials are usually guaranteed for transparency for up to10 years. These materials also have an advantage of being suitable for curved surfaces-polycarbonate being most bendable of the two materials.

The most suitable panel material depends on your needs as well as the conditions that prevail in your location. In this regard, you must also keep your budgetary constrains in mind. This best deal would only be the one that your pocket allows. the one that your pocket allows.

Choosing A Window Greenhouse

Winter season can often be gloomy and depressing, especially if you look out of your window, only to find defoliated plants and cold, dead flowerbeds. Not so long ago, these lifeless flowerbeds would have been covered with all sorts of wonderful and attractive flowers. However, by employing the concept of a window greenhouse, one can transform the dull outlook of your window into one displaying all sorts of colorful plants.

A window greenhouse can also find its utility with plant lovers with limited space.   A window greenhouse, also called a garden window, has a very small construction. Using this little garden you can enjoy see flowers blossom all round the year.

Before purchasing your garden window, factors such as cost, materials and the size of your window must be considered.

In the market, complete bay window kits are available that are both energy efficient and easy to install. Furthermore, these window greenhouses serve another purpose that is to increase the depth or "open up" your room.

Types of greenhouse windows

Generally two types of window greenhouses are readily available for you to choose from. These are bow greenhouse windows and bay greenhouse windows.

A bow type window greenhouse comprises of several glass segments give it a rounded look. On the other hand, bay greenhouse windows usually has three segments, whereby sides are angled at 30 or 45 degrees.

Of the various options available to you, the most economical option would be to utilize a complete kit of a bow-type greenhouse rather than building a new greenhouse yourself. In this case, all you need to do is to remove the existing window in your room, enlarge the opening according to the size mentioned in the manual and then simply install the greenhouse in place.

It would be wise to purchase a kit that matches the size of your existing window, so that additional labor involved with enlargement of the opening can be minimized. Furthermore, the size must also suit the plants that would populate your greenhouse. For starters, a smaller window greenhouse unit would be a better option. However for more open space you should go for a unit that offers greater depth.

Bow greenhouse windows made from vinyl or aluminum coated wood are quite attractive. The interior is made from natural wood or imitation wood. Usually stained or painted vinyl gives a real look and has the advantage of being maintenance-free.

While making a decision to purchase greenhouse you should select an insulated bow type greenhouse window. The glass paneling should be made from glass that has insulating spacer.

Placement

In order to select the best location, survey your home for the location having "ready-made" qualities that support your window greenhouse. These qualities include warmth, adequate sunlight and water access. Moreover, the location must be such that you have easy access to it, without causing hindrance to other activities in your home.

It is a good idea to buy flower pots and arrange them inside your greenhouse. In this way, you enjoy summer flowers during fall by planting them these pots. Herbs could be a useful addition to your greenhouse window as they are attractive, useful and fragrant.

By having a greenhouse window, you can now have the pleasure of gardening all year long, no matter what kind of weather prevails outside.

Enjoying Greenhouse Gardening

People spend their free time according to their interests. Some busy themselves with sports while others like culinary. People who love plants enjoy gardening. With the right kind of tools and equipment, plant lovers can beautify their home while enjoying their hobby.

The hobby of taking care of plants requires that you spend quite some time with you plants, watering them, preventing pests from harming them and removing weeds from your plants' vicinity. However, these activities could expose you to the sun for extended periods, causing sunburns. An alternative option that will protect you from over dose of sunlight, without compromising on your hobby is to have a greenhouse.

Construction of a greenhouse

A greenhouse is an enclosed structure that houses plants inside a controlled ambience for them to flourish. Its construction comprises of a framework with panels placed on the frame. The frame is made from either wood or metal. On the other hand, greenhouse panels, which form the walls and ceiling of the greenhouse, are made from glass or plastic. A typical greenhouse is a free standing structure. However, if not much space is available, then making an attachment to your house can do the trick. In this case, your greenhouse would simply be an additional room in your house.

Before you embark upon constructing the greenhouse, it is useful to check if complies with the building codes your locality. In simple words, you must be allowed to build your chosen design by the authorities. Deciding the location of your greenhouse is important and is dictated by the climate of your location. If it gets very hot during summer you might like to build the greenhouse under a tree for shade.

Constructing a greenhouse can be quite expensive. If buying a greenhouse kit, or having a contractor build one or you is beyond your means, it would be a good idea to set one up from scratch. After doing the necessary paperwork, you can start building one right away.

Post construction issues

Once you have a greenhouse, choosing the plants to cultivate in your greenhouse is the next step. This step requires some research. In this regard, one may like to consult the internet or visit the local gardening shop to do a survey.

Most people use greenhouses to growing flowering plants. This trend is now being replaced with being utilized for fruits and vegetables so that these can be made available all over the year. Furthermore, farming techniques are now being implemented into gardening .As a result, soil is not always used as a growth medium. However, water can also be used instead of soil. This technique is called hydroponics which essentially eliminates the problem of weeds, thus saving a lot of time and hassle.

The hobby of cultivating plants in a greenhouse can even reward you with handsome profits. Since the greenhouse enables you to grow fruits and vegetables all around the year, you could actually sell your produce during off seasons, when prices are high. For this purpose, all you need to do is to sell your harvest in a local grocery store.

Before setting up a greenhouse you must do a thorough research and be aware of your financial limits. This way you will be able to avoid problems and will truly enjoy your hobby.

Building An Easy And Cost-effective Greenhouse On Your Back Yard

Prior to embarking on your greenhouse project, you must do proper planning as this would save a lot of hassle as well as money. The design of your green would depend on your home's architecture, space, the plants that you plan to cultivate and the available budget. The greenhouse must be able to provide a suitable environment for the plants it is intended for.

Location

Since plants manufacture their food by using energy from sunlight, it is necessary that the greenhouse is located such that it receives ample amount of sunlight. Too much sunlight, however can be baneful for plants. In order to protect it from high intensity light, tree shade can prove to be quite beneficial. Deciduous trees such as oak and maple can provide adequate shade over a greenhouse thereby protecting its occupants from strong late afternoon sun in summers. Nevertheless, the location must be planned such that the shade does not block sunlight in the morning. Deciduous trees, unlike coniferous or other evergreen trees, automatically permit sunlight during winters, since they defoliate in that season. Evergreen trees are thus not preferable to shelter greenhouses.

The site you plan to erect your greenhouse on must have good drainage. This can be achieved by constructing it on high ground. Improper drainage will cause water logging, which cause plants to decay.

Construction

To construct a greenhouse for your home, you would need a sheet of Universal Canopy, around 10 x 20 feet in size. You would also need 6 mil clear plastic roll, about 20 x 100 feet in size, 4 to 8 T-Posts, 15 to 20 Squeeze Clips, 18 Ratcheting Tie-downs, 1 roll duck tape, 3 rolls Heavy Duty 3M Clear Tape. You could also include heaters, fans, and gro-lights as an option.

Once you have the aforementioned paraphernalia, you could proceed by following the guideline given below:

1. First of all, set up your frame, and as you insert each piece wrap the connection point with 2 or 3 rounds of Duck Tape.

2. Next, attach the Tie downs by staggering all of them evenly over the top of the frame. Make the straps tight, but don't bare down and over tighten.

3. Use at least 4 T-post to anchor the 4 corners of the greenhouse. Place the T-post on the inside an drive at least 12" in the ground. then wrap at least the top 24" with Duck Tape to secure and eliminate any sharp edges.

4. Now splice two sheets of plastic in order to achieve full coverage. (unless you found bigger plastic) Cut 2 pieces of plastic at 30 feet. this will give you two, 20' x 30' pieces. You will splice the 30' sections, giving you one big sheet of 38' x 30'.

5. Allow the plastic to touch the ground on the end caps, but if your overlap was to much and it won't reach the ground on both ends. However you can make your own end caps or doors with the extra plastic.

6. Use the clips to attach the plastic to the pipe legs. Clip everywhere you think it needs it. Any tears caused by the clips can be fixed with heavy duty clear tape.

Once you have successfully followed all the aforementioned steps you have constructed your very own greenhouse. Congratulations!

Greenhouses On The Move

Greenhouses are fast becoming popular with plant lovers. Because of the benefits a greenhouse has to offer, more and more hobbyists are considering on having one in their homes. However, most people are likely change residence for a number of reasons, including better job opportunities. Since a full-sized greenhouses would be impractical to relocate, such people can make use of portable types.

Portable greenhouses, are required to be light weight so that they are easy to transfer. Furthermore, they must be compact, east to setup and dismantle. In fact most portable greenhouse kits can be erected with in 30 minutes. Being compact, these greenhouses can be easily stored in a convenient location, such as a garage or in a closet when not in used.

Purpose

In terms of functionality, portable greenhouses are required to trap sunlight within their enclosure, making use of the greenhouse effect. This is exactly what is required of a regular greenhouse. However, in addition to this a portable greenhouse is required to be light weight and easy to commission.

Usefulness

Portable greenhouses are well suited for early plantation of seeds, protection of tender plants from cold weather and growing different plants species not commonly found in the area.

Popularity

The popularity of portable greenhouses in on the rise among gardeners. This is primarily due to the fact that these models set up quite quickly and easily. Furthermore, they can be pulled down within no time, allowing the space to be used for some other purpose. Thus the space occupied by a portable greenhouse does not get locked up, but remains available.

Portable greenhouses are also recommended for beginners since this will allow them hands on experience on a greenhouse before they decide to build a full-sized one. To top it all, portable hothouses are also inexpensive to setup as well as to maintain. As a result, first timers can begin their gardening without spending large sums of money to purchase parts needed to setup a full-scale greenhouse. Moreover, since their installation is faster and easier than regular ones so no advanced tools or expertise is required.

Types of portable greenhouses

Portable greenhouses are available in various shapes and sizes. They could be in the form of a small tent in which only 2 plant shelves can be placed. Others may look like portable closets, about 6 feet tall. Bigger models, around 7 to 8 feet high are also available. These larger greenhouses can accommodate up to 3 to 4 larger shelves within.

Operating a portable greenhouse

Weather conditions can fluctuate rapidly. Keep an eye on the weather report that is available on the internet or broadcast on your local radio and television. During sudden cold spells cover the greenhouse at night with leaves filled sacks for insulation. This would prevent the ambience inside from getting cold. .

During hot spells, on the other hand, the portable greenhouse can be moved to a shady location. Alternately, some form of covering can be used over the frame to prevent sunlight from being transmitted inside.

Portable greenhouses would be useful for both amateur gardeners as well as professional ones. Their portability allows you to transport it to a more convenient location. Furthermore, Its maintenance is not as costly as in the case with permanent, full-sized ones. As a result, every one stands to benefit from a portable greenhouse.

Download 100+ Books
Completely Free!
No Hassles...
No Charges...
Just Click And Download
100% Free!
CLICK HERE

This Product Is Brought To You By